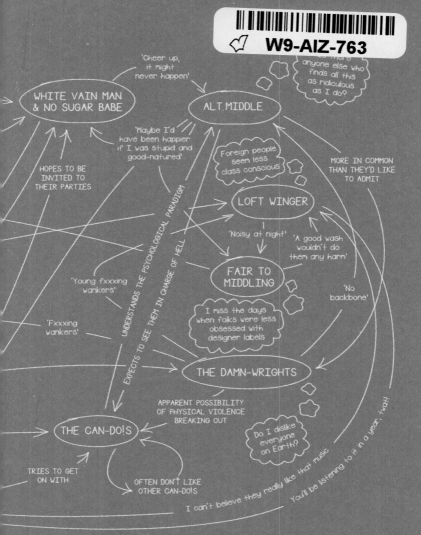

THE
MIDDLE CLASS
HANDBOOK

An illustrated field guide to the behaviour and tastes
of Britain's new middle-class tribes

NOT ACTUAL SIZE

The Middle Class Handbook
Published by Not Actual Size

Copyright ©2010 Not Actual Size

ISBN 978-0-9565712-0-5

Not Actual Size
3-4 Bartholomew Place
London
EC1A 7HH

www.notactualsize.co.uk

CONTENTS

FOREWORD

If the people of this book really exist, really represent something, trending and blending away as they do, you could have absolutely called the May 2010 Election. It's all about how you deal with the last slice of pizza (see Page 34).

When I was in my first job, as a Boy Market Research Executive (in Lower Belgrave St, SW1, absolutely not Hanger Lane Gyratory territory), we were all excited by psychographics – the idea that quantifying people's attitudes – and creating clusters from them that described interesting new groupings, people cast free from the old inadequate categories of notional NRS class A to E – would enable you to build lifelike segmentations that could help your clients sell things with pinpoint accuracy.

The problem was that when most practitioners – ad agency planners, research companies' special teams – put up these groupings they looked about as compelling and convincing as a Cabbage Patch doll. You could always work back from the stereotypes with their silly names to those familiar hard realities of age, education and occupation – to social determinism. All that social mobility, all that self-definition hadn't really happened yet outside a few London boroughs. But factor in the massive increase in higher education since then and all that hierarchy of experience, all those goods and services pioneered and then gone mass, all those opportunities for niche brands built around planners' Big Ideas; all that masstige and all those defining tiny luxuries (Green & Black's, Ben & Jerry's) all those High Concept Retailers, all that stuff did the business. The 21st century turned anyone with a pulse and a reasonable credit-card status into a Shopping Centre Connoisseur with the urge for self-definition, ideally through something creative.

So you get a set of groupings like this lot, amusingly written, obsessive about brands, observant in a novelist's way about small behaviours (10 ways with that last slice of pizza, six dinner-party hand-signals between husband and wife) and not only could you make a reasonable case for it now, you could also make a game.

As middle-class people did more getting and spending and experiencing they became more observant themselves. They've become vastly more sophisticated about group-spotting. Ann Barr and I first did our bit in the early 1980s with *The Sloane Ranger Handbook* and a raft of Handbooks followed. And people started doing it for themselves and arguing the toss. Indeed I'd say it's the defining characteristic of modern middle-classness to want to play it. Neither the old upper class, the global plutocrats, nor the underclass are much bothered by this game. Old uppers feel, like Maudie Littlehampton, "If it's me, it's U", and global plutocrats aren't into small behaviours; they go for giant. And the underclass are focused on fantastical luck rather than on any thought-through social mobility strategies.

With the *Middle Class Handbook* you don't have to shout at the printed page (as in "no X would ever do/ buy Y"). You can share it, debate it and demonstrate your fantastically-nuanced grasp of modern aspiration online. It's all very nuanced in the *MCH*, as in the confused Loft Wingers who used to ape a just-backdated collection of prole styles, but have started losing the faith now.

I love this stuff. I could talk to you for hours about it, particularly about the way the authors get a fair bit of it right. My only criticism is the Get a Life one; the people in these groupings are so busy defining and expressing themselves through brands, compounding it with small behaviours and lots of attitudinising, they must all be exhausted.

Peter York

INTRODUCTION

What does it mean to be middle class in Britain in 2010? Does it mean you drive an Audi, live in Surrey, holiday in Puglia, shop at Boden and send Zak and Evie to tennis lessons in the summer holidays? Or that you have a 4x4, live in Alderley Edge, have a holiday home on the Bulgarian coast and employ private tutors for the kids in the hope of getting them into a good grammar? Or is it, in fact, all a great deal more nuanced and complicated than that?

Does it mean, for example, that you read the tabloid *Times* but not the *Daily Mirror*? That you might wear a fashionable trilby, but steer well clear of baseball caps? That you call the lavatory "the euphemism", and actually quite like the sound of "restroom"? Does it make a difference if you call dinner "supper" or supper "tea" or lunch "dinner", or if you combine meals and go out with friends for brunch on Sundays? Are bankers middle class? Are bloggers? Twitterers? What about Secret Millionaires, or public sector workers? Do politics come into it? If so, who is the more middle – Clegg, or Cameron? Diane Abbott, or Ann Widdecombe?

Are Range Rovers middle class?

Is it acceptable to discuss house prices?

David Lammy, or cheeky old Lembit Opik? *The Middle Class Handbook* exists to consider such questions, and to identify the sub-tribes into which Britain's modern middle classes divide themselves.

It started out six years ago as a series of conversations between friends and workmates whose jobs involved reading a lot of market research and information about consumer demographics. Feeling that much of this material was a bit dry and unhelpful when it came to understanding what people really felt about themselves and each other, we began compiling our own alternative, tongue-in-cheek guide to consumer tribes, based on a mixture of research and our own experience. We printed it in a small book called *Class of 2004/5*, sent this to some colleagues and journalists, and some of the latter ran stories about it. A few years later, after some of us had left the agency, and then met up again through a new one, Not Actual Size, we turned the idea into a blog about modern middle-class life in Britain, www.middleclasshandbook.co.uk. After people began joining us there to debate crucial issues such as why

Posh?

Posh?

middle-class couples talk about each other after visiting each other's homes and how to divide up the last pizza slice, we decided to publish a new and more detailed version, which is what you are now holding.

So what, to come back to our earlier question, do we mean by middle class? Do we middle-class British people really know who we are nowadays? Do we really have anything in common, apart from our shared love of Alan Bennett, high consumption of coffee and obsession with the value of our homes?

In the past year or so, the values and tastes that the middle classes do or do not share have been vigorously debated. Politicians have designated the middle as a key battleground, and analysts, journalists and authors have sought to define and categorise it. They conclude that the UK's middle class is growing, although they are not sure if it is yet the majority. They note that unemployment, wage stagnation, low social mobility and public sector cutbacks mean that many of its members feel anxious and embattled; they also note that as a result, it is growing angry, with the Ministry of Defence warning that the middle class

Numbers and definitions can be tricky

Hands up if you think you're middle class

could become a source of dangerous revolutionaries in the next 30 years. The striking thing about that particular prediction is surely that while three years ago it would have seemed like a joke, it now seems credible. Any discussion of current middle class-ness has in the background a mood of deep insecurity, unease and uncertainty.

Definitions of these potential revolutionaries remain problematic, though, because most people do not define themselves in the ways that researchers do. Virtually no one in the UK, for example, admits to being upper class at all.

The truth seems to be that we are caught between definitions of middle class; between a behavioural one based on traditional British notions of gentility, respectability, and manners, and a simple economic definition of the middle as simply neither super-rich nor poverty-level poor. That's a lot of people, of course, but within that there are dozens, perhaps hundreds of sub-tribes; and while Britain's middle-class tribes once defined themselves by social background, education and job, these days the

Chintz: acceptable?

Coffee: complex

defining is more dependent on taste, behaviour, brand loyalties and consumer choices.

Middle class-ness could be seen as a matter of having good manners and trying to say The Right Thing in polite company – but then where would that leave Jeremy Clarkson and his fans? Or Melanie Phillips? Or Charlotte Church? It could be a question of reserved demeanour and conservative tastes – but then what of Jamie Oliver, or Gok Wan, or Victoria Beckham? And of course it could be an issue of income, between £30,000 and £250,000, say – but then what about all the out-of-work finance managers who have learned to replace champers with M&S Prosecco until the recession's over?

You can think of this book as a handy reference guide to the myriad ways in which we can be middle class in Britain today. And let's face it, most of us could use a guide – because in our interconnected and overheated consumer universe, it is rather hard to keep track of all our shifting tastes.

On the one hand, we all share a common pop culture. We all work too hard, we're all interested in

Anger: growing

Pizza: significant

international food and drink, we all watch American TV, we're all prone to a bit of New-Agey claptrap, we all think about our hairstyles too much and the world around us too little. On the other hand, we find infinite ways to express ourselves through the things we do and buy and say. Do you undo one button, or two? Do you say, "Could I have" or "Can I get"? Are you ashamed or proud of buying from Boden?

This book looks at the crucial details, and offers a classification system based on them. The diagram on Page 82 shows how the different groups get along. How do you know you are middle class in the first place, though? That takes us back to our original question: what does it mean to be middle class in Britain in 2010? The one thing that links all middle class people is anxiety and/or curiosity about their status; being middle class means always wondering what kind of middle class you are. Once you have asked that, there is no going back.

The editors

JAMIE OLIVER'S ARMY

Matt and Steph came of age as the young, optimistic middle-class foot soldiers of Blair's Britain. In recent years they have come to feel overworked, put-upon and rather taken for granted by bosses, politicians and extended family but have responded by working harder and making the best of things. They still quietly apply themselves with great vigour to their chief objective of making life just a bit (Matt and Steph use the words "Just a bit" quite a lot) more individual, fun and interesting. As this has become just a bit more difficult in the past year, they have found comfort in their ambitions; now in their late twenties, they think a lot about their next career move. When they talk about their lives, another phrase that crops up often is, "At the moment, but what I'd/we'd really like is" (or for our purposes ATMBWIRLI).

Matt works as a designer for a company that produces marketing materials (ATMBWIRLI to draw a comic), and Steph works as an instructor at a local gym (ATMBWIRLI to be an estate agent) two days a week. She went back a few months ago after having

WHERE TO SPOT JAMIE OLIVER'S ARMY

1 New medium-sized housing developments in satellite towns
2 Villages within 20 minutes of medium-sized cities
3 Outer suburbs
4 In the garden having barbecues with parents and neighbours
5 Local soft play centre with the kids

Steph loves soft play because it's safe

HOW TO SPOT JAMIE OLIVER'S ARMY

- Retro T-shirts
- Ted Baker tops
- G-Star denim
- Ford S-Max
- Well-used copy of Jamie's America
- Box of stuff near PC at home for putting on eBay
- Quirky home decor

Matt's favourite doormat, ever

their first baby, George. She would have stayed at home with him full time, but Matt's hours have been cut, and to be honest they're worried about his job. The upshot is Steph's mum now has George on Mondays and Tuesdays. It works OK although she and her mum disagree about George's diet.

Matt and Steph always thought unemployment wouldn't be a problem if you were willing to work hard; now they feel shaken, and a bit scared although they don't tell anyone. It's not just about having too little money; they are both great planners (holidays, days out, parties, Christmases – sometimes Steph even talks about where they might live after retiring), and so it was looking forward and planning special events that took their minds off shortcomings in their lifestyles. Now, without the plans, they have to

HOLLY TREE CROFT

Matt's unpublished comic strip is based on his life with Steph in a fictional new housing development called *Holly Tree Croft*. Fusing reality with sci-fi and fantasy, it features Matt living a double life as put-upon husband and secret superhero Mattman. The real Matt and Steph sometimes joke about the day "when Steven Spielberg buys the comic".

Zoe is Matt's cool friend's girlfriend, and she is staying over en route to London. But she has made a sarcastic remark about their kitchen design.

ATMBWIRLI

Times are hard for Matt and Steph, but they can still dream. Their key 2010 catchphrase is *at the moment, but what I'd really like is*, or ATMBWIRLI

MATT

Commercial designer ATMBWIRLI to do my own comic

Planning on the Algarve ATMBWIRLI to go on an elephant safari holiday in Bali

Converting the loft ATMBWIRLI to design our own house from scratch

Ford S-Max ATMBWIRLI a Lambretta SX200

Have tickets to see Snow Patrol live at the O2 Arena ATMBWIRLI to see them play at Glastonbury

STEPH

Gym instructor ATMBWIRLI to be a successful estate agent

Planning on the Algarve ATMBWIRLI a luxury beach holiday in Bali

Selling bits I pick up on eBay ATMBWIRLI to have my own interiors shop

Clio ATMBWIRLI a new Mini

Talking about going to Glastonbury ATMBWIRLI a mini break, to somewhere with a spa

live with these shortcomings. Their compensation for not being able to plan is "little treats"; this year these have included luxury chocolate bars, premium ice cream, a home spa kit for Steph and the two-disc special edition of *Goodfellas* for Matt to watch on the widescreen with friends and a beer.

One of Jamie Oliver's Army's greatest talents is making commonplace things special – visiting friends chuckle at their Saturday Chinese takeaway nights, when Steph gets the Chinese bowls out and the food HAS to be ordered in time for the start of *The X Factor* or *Britain's Got Talent* (she sometimes lets George stay up to watch them – he picked the winners last time round!). This ability to transform the mundane through sheer enthusiasm in part explains their tremendous affection for upmarket

THINGS THAT JAMIE OLIVER'S ARMY HAVE IN THEIR HOME

- One wall of feature wallpaper
- Family portraits on three canvases
- Ceramic tiles on external wall as garden feature
- Retro push-button telephone handset
- Tableware with word prints
- Advertising sign bearing one of their names
- Three-seater brown leather sofa
- Mongolian wool cushions
- Large dark-wood Jali coffee table
- Terracotta and gold colour scheme
- Objects with names: Matt and Steph name not only the car but also the fridge (Jeremiah), buggy (Jacquetta) and various other, smaller items. The names make sense only to them, but they like explaining why they allocated them

The barbecue is "Phil". It's a long story

She'd call it Dougal

shopping malls. They were excited to visit London's Westfield recently. Matt thought the parking system was amazing.

The transformation-through-attitude principle also, of course, applies to Jamie Oliver, the man who captures the essence of Matt and Steph's take on life in the way he fuses anti-establishment individuality with something as basic as cooking. Matt and Steph were first drawn to Jamie by the brilliant way he cooked novel versions of familiar foods like burgers or sandwiches. However, more recently, they would say that the reason they respect him is that he "puts something back". Matt and Steph have an immense respect for people who do things to put something back, or try to help other people. This sometimes motivates them to take on jobs like helping Steph's

So unlucky

Top bloke

mum with the church Christmas fair or old people's summer tea, although invariably this becomes a bit of a bind, and they regret saying they'd help.

They have also discovered a new delight in pseudo-traditional things; they don't know if it's them getting old (it isn't, it's looking for the comfort and security of the past during an economic downturn, says Matt's left-wing friend from college. Steph thinks he talks rubbish, and his wife is snotty) but they just really love all that stuff like old-fashioned sweet shops, teashops, and even some of that Cath Kidston kitchenware, though Steph is not keen on the flowery stuff. (The years in marketing have dulled Matt's sense of absurdity, but Steph thinks, privately, there is too much trendiness for the sake of it nowadays.)

Another change in Matt and Steph's tastes in the past five years is a greater predilection for unusual experiences, and socialising outside the home. The money that in 2005 they would have spent on a novelty wall hanging is now used for tickets to a big one-off gig or a visit to a novelty restaurant. Jamie Oliver's Army is responsible for much of what is new in the style-conscious hedonistic parts of the leisure industry. Big gigs, festivals, trendy shopping centres, the girls' and boys' nights out that have grown out of 1990s stag and hen culture: Matt and Steph helped to make them all. Excuses for a really big bash are always welcome, and they're both already planning something special for their thirtieths – something really different, maybe a weekend away with the girls/boys. They love doing things "with the girls" and "with the boys" – hence Steph going to see Take That, and Matt playing poker. However, they do still

MATT'S ALL-TIME FAVOURITE TEES

OSAKA
6

DAVE'S STAG

MEXICO86

Bought it at Bluewater | Designed it himself | He's addicted to eBay

HEROES

MATT
♥ Peter Kaye ♥ Richard Hammond ♥ Ben Stiller ♥ Guy Ritchie in a strange way ♥ Lewis Hamilton ♥ Vince Vaughn ♥ Dizzee Rascal ♥ Mike Myers ♥ Frank Miller ♥ Jackie Chan

STEPH
♥ Kate Garraway (for the clothes) ♥ Amanda Holden ♥ Sophie Kinsella ♥ Julia Roberts ♥ Jennifer Aniston ♥ Leona Lewis ♥ Jo Frost

AWFUL

✗ Kerry Katona ✗ Jordan ✗ WAGs ✗ Gordon Ramsay ✗ John Prescott ✗ Jonathan Ross ✗ Angelina Jolie

"MUST-SEE"

★ Come Dine With Me ★ Four Weddings ★ Jamie – of course! ★ The X Factor and Britain's Got Talent ★ Wild At Heart ★ MTV ★ Hell's Kitchen ★ Lazytown with George

STEPH'S GOLDEN RULE OF GOOD TASTE

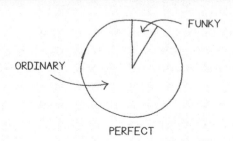

FUNKY

ORDINARY

PERFECT

SHOPPING CENTRES THAT JAMIE OLIVER'S ARMY LOVES TO VISIT

Matt and Steph love shopping centres, and reject the idea that the shops are all the same. They point out that the stock in the M&S in, say, Newcastle differs to that in a big M&S in London – finding the new lines is where the fun lies. They also really like food courts, and cheerfully joke that they would happily visit London's Westfield for its food and futuristic computerised parking system alone.

1 Westfield, London
2 Trafford Centre, Manchester
3 Bluewater, Kent
4 Metro Centre, Newcastle
5 The Gyle, Edinburgh
6 Highcross Leicester
7 Sprucefield, Lisburn
8 Princesshay, Exeter

Manchester

Leicester

Newcastle

go out together of course – last year they went to a music festival together for the first time. Steph wasn't that bothered, but Matt enjoyed it. They're going to see Kings of Leon soon, and next they'd really like to try Jongleurs comedy club.

Holidays have changed, too. They used to go to amazing coupley places, but last year it was a villa with Steph's mum and dad. Every now and again they try out a British holiday – they've done Cornwall, the Lakes, Dorset – but it's just as dear as going abroad and secretly Steph likes a tan. This year they got a brilliant deal to Croatia.

In the main, holidays are like the other activities that Matt and Steph enjoy. The trips themselves are not out of the ordinary, but they undertake them in ways that show they have a bit of individuality and

SOCIAL NETWORKING WITH MATT & STEPH

 Steph Jamie-Olivers-Army bored of my usual wines and fancy a change, got any recommendations? The more the better!
Yesterday at 15:05 · Comment · Like

 Louise Bluewater Wolf Blass Merlot is nice
Yesterday at 20:49

 James Trafford I like a bit of Turning Leaf
Yesterday at 21:30

 Chris Spricefield Blossom Hill beats JC anyday
4 hours ago

 Wendy Gyle I like Wolf Blass Shiraz but Banrock Station do a better Merlot. We bought a case of it!
3 hours ago

Steph loves Facebook, and she uses it in the way she used to use her stream of text messages – to offer a commentary on, and to invite others to add chat about, many of the details of her life. She will post to say she is about to clean the house, to announce that Matt is out and she is about to crack open the Ewan McGregor DVD, or to ask anyone if they have any suggestions for a new wine for her to try. Matt spends far less time than his wife on social networking sites. He used to have a MySpace page that he used to showcase his art, but he let that drift and isn't even sure if it's up any more. Now he has his own site, which needs updating – and he uses Facebook a bit to keep in touch with friends. His favourite site is a graphic design forum, on which people sometimes mention jobs that may be going – the harsh fact of life is that he needs to keep an eye on that sort of thing at the moment.

creativity – "funkiness", as Steph calls it. This is why they had a Routemaster bus to transport guests at their wedding, and why, when shopping for George, they will seek out the wackier things in babyGap while avoiding Mothercare. When Steph finally gets enough money to change her car, she wants to swap the Clio for a Mini because you can customise them (she's already planned a colour scheme, of course).

The principle of ordinary-with-a-twist runs deep with Matt and Steph. Their aspirations for their children are in some ways timeless – they want them

JAMIE OLIVER'S ARMY SUB-TRIBES

NEW YOUNG FOGEY CLUB

Henry and Chloe. Live in Edwardian terraced house in affluent areas of West Country town. Management consultants. Aged 26, act 62, but not nostalgic; see their take on conservatism as the future. Keen on badminton and cycling, active charity volunteers.
Role models: Louise Bagshawe & Prince William

THE EUPPIES

Marco and Jana. Live in flat in outer suburb. Marco has fledgling courier business, Jana primary school teacher. Moved from Hungary four years ago. Ambitious, eager to "assimilate", aspire to Boden lifestyle. Make point of speaking English to each other in public as a gesture of politeness and dislike fellow new arrivals who draw undue attention to themselves.
Role models: Sian Williams & Richard Hammond

WIINAGERS

Keith and Pat. Live in semi-detached house in modern housing development in small town. Keith an accountant, Pat a midwife. Keenly involved in community/social activities, and especially in their grown-up children's lives; endlessly organising trips with extended family in which grandparents are experts on the Wii. Ageless and casual, bit like Gap chinos.
Role models: Sharon Osbourne & Mark Horton

FOCUSED MAN & WOMAN

Phil and Laura. Live in large semi in prosperous outer suburbs. Both work for multinationals, where they have achieved senior positions with a discipline that they also apply to domestic life. Love endurance sport; it imposes order on things. "What," they ask, "is the point of life without achievements?"
Role models: Chris Hoy & Paula Radcliffe

to be well behaved, well mannered, and kind – but, far more than their parents, they would also like their kids to be creative. More than anything, it's this creativity and individuality stuff that differentiates Matt and Steph from their solidly middle-class mum and dad's generation. Both sets of parents aimed to appear respectable, reliable and reasonably well-off but Matt and Steph, while not rejecting those values entirely, also see kudos in self-expression – though they are wary of anything so out of the ordinary that it might invite ridicule. Creativity and individuality are important to them, but they also like the neighbours to think their house looks neat and tidy.

THE HORNBY SET

The best way of describing Jonathon and Claire is to say that their friends who are not members of The Hornby Set find visits to their house pleasant enough (Jonathon does the cooking, and always comes up with some incredibly elaborate stuff) yet somehow exhausting. Why? Because every detail of everything you do/eat/look at has a complex significance that has to be explained to you.

Jonathon and Claire avoid your kind of olive oil, for instance, because while it *says* Italian, unless you buy single estate, the olives are probably imported from Spain and merely *pressed* in Italy. That photograph of Steve Hillage at Glastonbury in 1979 is in fact a limited edition, and reminds them of when you could smoke dope at the festival without undercover cops arresting you. Farrow & Ball is so class-ridden, with its obsession with old stately homes. Jonathon even likes talking cars now that they have greener engines, and go a decent speed (they were always going to buy a Prius but ended up getting an Audi; now they have a Lexus RX 450h).

There is a reason for this. Jonathon and Claire

Jonathon spent 18 months and three weeks researching bikes

are the descendents of the old 1970s and 1980s
radical left-wingers who believed everything you
did was political. As students at sit-ins and demos
they confirmed each other's conviction that the
clothes you wore and even the food you ate was
bound up with the global capitalist conspiracy.
When they decided to give up on the revolution
and change things from within, setting up ethical
businesses or taking executive roles in the public
sector, they carried on their politics through these
consumer choices. There was a certain middle-class
competitiveness to it all as well, of course. The
Hornby Set are the people, more than any other, who
invested environmentally-friendly products with the
sort of green-upmanship that alienated sceptics.

This obsession with their consumer choices means

THERE'S NO APP FOR THAT

Jonathon and Claire love both their iPhones and money-making schemes. No surprise then that since reading about people making money from apps, they have been designing some of their own.

EatHere

EatHere identifies your position and shows a list of local food producers within a specified range. Has filters for organic, free-range etc. Ideal for weekend cottage owners; Jonathon can't believe it doesn't exist already.

Untourist

For travellers and holiday-makers; identifies your position and lists nearby beaches, restaurants, and bars that are undiscovered by tourists. Luka and Sam point out obvious flaw, and call parents "snobs, basically".

Ling-au-pair

Dictionary translating English to languages spoken by au pairs and nannies. Would include phrases such as "Sorry it's short notice but can you work late tonight?" and "What was it like to live under communism?"

iSalute

Simply shows a clenched fist rising to show solidarity with people in struggle around the world. Bit like iPint, but serious. Their children Luka and Sam think "it's about the Vietnam war… or something".

They've gone right off him

they feel compelled to know about everything; they love to appear to be polymaths, although genuinely polymath friends suspect they are "wiki-llectuals", i.e they sometimes seem to swot up on the internet in order to drop facts into conversation. They always read all the information they are given at an exhibition even though they are bored by it; they comment on political blogs (usernames: Gangof_1 and Trot55) and cite things they have looked up on Wikipedia as if they actually knew them; and they love the way Stephen Fry and people in *The West Wing* seem to know so much. Their home offices are crammed with books that have been lent to them by others in the Hornby Set, just as they have lent theirs. "You must read this," they say. "You'll love it!"

"Right, I will."

REALLY LOVE

Barack & Michelle
Dizzee Rascal
Richard Hawley
Jon Cruddas
Roberto Bolano
Hilary Mantel
George Monbiot
Hugh Fearnley-Whittingstall
Lily Allen
Sam Taylor-Wood
Charlie Brooker

DON'T LIKE

Richard Littlejohn
Gordon Ramsay
The Saturdays
Dan Brown
George Osborne
Sky Sports presenters
Holly Willoughby
Michael McIntyre
Nadine Dorries
Boris Johnson
Stephenie Meyer

NOT SURE

Gok Wan
Katy Perry
John Mackey
Andy McNab
Bono
Caroline Flint
Russell Brand
Bob Crow
Kelly Osbourne
Audrey Niffenegger
Thierry Henry

Of course no one ever does. They read the first few pages and a plot summary online, and bluff.

A few years ago, Jonathon and Claire really felt they had arrived. They vaguely knew some of the people in the Labour government (including one cabinet minister who used to go on sit-ins with Claire. He was a dyed-in-the-wool Maoist in those days – Claire says she won't tell but always spills the beans after a second glass of Malbec), and it seemed to represent more or less what they thought. The Hornby Set ideas seemed the Right Ideas – and they made good money. There were the two well-timed property deals. A pay rise for Jonathon when he masterminded a new, talked-about programme of social interventions with his public-sector organisation. The mail-order wholefoods business

WHAT'S ON THE HORNBY SET'S OLIVE OIL LABEL?

1. Caption referring to the Fairtrade co-operative that produced the oil
2. Reverse: lengthy biography of the Fairtrade co-operative that produced the oil, with details of the area in which the olives were grown, written in straightforward English without post-Innocent drinks childlike tone, which The Hornby Set now considers done to death and suspect
3. Country of origin (Palestine: olive trees are not actually native to Italy, Jonathon likes to tell guests)
4. Picture of single-estate olive grove belonging to co-operative
5. Fairtrade logo (actually The Hornby Set think fair trade is suspect as trade undermines local food supply. However, Nabali olives are indigenous to Palestine, so that's ok)
6. GMO free
7. Guide to taste and aroma of the oil
8. Biodynamic
9. Cold pressed (not for cooking then!)
10. Signature of presser, details of mill and date of pressing
11. Hand-picked olives (more expensive, but the harvesting machines bruise the olives, which ruins them)
12. Rousing, semi-political slogan

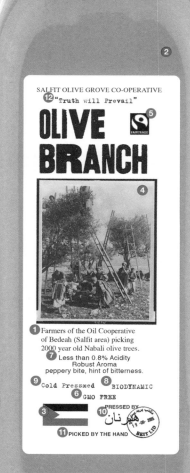

SALFIT OLIVE GROVE CO-OPERATIVE
(12) "Truth will Prevail"

OLIVE BRANCH

(5) FAIRTRADE

(4)

(1) Farmers of the Oil Cooperative of Bedeah (Salfit area) picking 2000 year old Nabali olive trees.
(7) Less than 0.8% Acidity
Robust Aroma
peppery bite, hint of bitterness.
(9) Cold Pressed   (8) BIODYNAMIC
(6) GMO FREE
(3)   (10) PRESSED BY
(11) PICKED BY THE HAND

ACCEPTABLE TV

The Wire
Question Time
Anything on BBC Four

UNACCEPTABLE TV

Cribs
Hollyoaks
How To Look Good Naked

THINGS THE HORNBY SET CHILDREN LIKE THAT THEIR PARENTS HATE

1 Xbox
2 McDonald's
3 All Saints
4 Nuts
5 Confessions of a Shopaholic
6 WAGs
7 Mockney accents

Luka blamed Xbox rage

YES PLEASE

Lexus
Leon restaurants
Penguin
BBC Four
Pralus chocolate
Apple
Tom's of Maine
First Direct
Whistles
Ocado
People Tree
Habitat

NO THANKS

Tesco
RBS
Primark
McDonald's
Bernard Matthews
Nestlé
Asda
Sky
ITV
Disney
dfs
Land of Leather

ON THE SHELF: ON AVERAGE, HOW FAR DID THE HORNBY SET ACTUALLY GET WITH THE FOLLOWING?

Wolf Hall over half

Failed States page 10

White Tiger page 30

2666 still hasn't started

The God Delusion finished

The Rest Is Noise halfway

Claire ran, with the help of a couple of *fantastic* Latvian girls, boomed. It meant they could move again into the catchment area for a good state school for their children, Luka and Sam. Everything seemed right.

Things feel a bit different now. Despite Claire's belief that people would keep spending on quality during a recession, takings are well down, and Inga has had to be let go. Thankfully Jonathon's wage can look after the both of them, but they can sense their friends' resentment sometimes ("Please don't let the conversation get on to bloody pensions again," they tell each before dinner parties).

And then there is the Luka and Sam problem. Jonathon and Claire are a little horrified and scared by their children. They encouraged them to do arty

31

THE HORNBY SET SUB-TRIBES

GOOD LIFERS
Will and Sarah. Live in large, detached period house in the countryside and own several acres of land, plus, possibly, livestock. Moved out from city and balance limited self-sufficiency with portfolio careers. Some locals were hostile when they were elected to parish council and came up with radical ideas for improving village life, but older urban friends are jealous. *Role models: Jimmy Doherty & Michaela Furney*

FREE WHELANS
Al and Polly. Live in townhouse in inner suburbs, with holiday cottage in UK or southern Europe. Veteran, non-Blairite left-wingers who cut their teeth on Sixties' radicalism and remain committed to the cause, working in senior roles in the public sector and trade unions make the Hornby Set (whom they dislike) feel guilty. *Role models: Jack Dromey & Harriet Harman*

SUBWAY SECT
Ben and Ellie. Recent graduates, renting shared house in outer suburbs. Combine career in creative/media sectors with part-time, low-paid work they hate, most commonly in fast-food industry. Generally dress down, and highly averse to everything they consider snobbish or pretentious. *Role models: Dave Grohl & Krissi Murison*

THE FUNANCIAL SECTOR
Rav and Jo. Live in large flat in inner suburbs, travel a great deal. Work in finance, but healthy salary and low outgoings – they have fairly simple tastes – fund frequent participation in arts, creative and leisure-based enterprises. Often sit on boards of arts organisations. Friends secretly try to guess how much money they actually have. *Role models: Diana Jenkins & Ivan Massow*

and altruistic activities. They used to eat Jonathon and Claire's food, and check out the urban nature reserves they had donated to, all that sort of thing; now Luka and Sam are teenagers, though, their chief interests are as far removed from that sort of thing as possible.

Jonathon and Claire are not *square* parents – they're on Facebook and Twitter (though Jonathon never checks his), and last year they really got into *The X Factor*, actually. Claire keeps up with fashion too, but she can't understand why Sam likes that badly-made rubbish – though she doesn't go to Primark, thank God. And at least she has an interest in clothes. All Luka wears are things that look a million sizes too big. They know he also smokes quite a lot of dope; they are hoping to contain this by being liberal, but they're not sure. It has reopened some old arguments about the school; Claire always said they should send them private, but Jonathon made her feel guilty about it.

As for the old Labour government – they gave up on them when it all came out about the Iraq war, and then the mess in Afghanistan; one thing you can say for the Hornbys is that they have a genuine moral repulsion for war – it is where their sentimentality about "the People" and their slightly showy rebellion has its sweet spot. They have washed their hands of the Labour Party now; secretly they are more comfortable with the coalition in as it means they can enjoy slagging off the government again – though what it will mean for Jonathon they just don't know. It's very much a "what-now?" moment, actually. Like all the modern middle classes, they replaced ideals with the principle of doing the best they could, and that seemed to do them very well for a while. Now, however, they feel as if they need another big idea.

THE POLITE SLICE

"Shared dining" has created a modern middle-class dilemma; who takes the last bit? With pizza in particular, one's approach to the problem tends to reveal one's class...

THE LIBERAL ACTUALLYS
Emily offers last slice around twice. On second set of polite refusals, Giles becomes exasperated, grabs the pizza and eats it in two mouthfuls, to withering looks from Emily.

THE HORNBY SET
No one eats it, and neither Jonathon nor Claire forces the issue as gluttony is frowned upon. Jonathon may get up to compost it.

THE DAMN-WRIGHTS
Jeremy and Carol order their own pizzas, so no tension arises. "What's the bloody point of choosing a topping you like and then having to swap it for pizza you'd never choose?" barks Jeremy.

THE LOFT WINGERS
Only Anna is affected by the polite-slice dilemma, as after two slices Tom and his friends will revert to his MacBook to listen to THAT mix. All girls will decline the slice, and Anna will have it for breakfast.

THE FAIR TO MIDDLINGS
All are paralysed by decorum, so polite slice remains to the end of the meal. Sylvia places it in triangular container from Lakeland, puts container in fridge until pizza goes stale, then feeds to birds.

THE CHAVEAU RICHES
Extremely unlikely to experience dilemma, as they always order roughly twice the amount of pizza they need.

JAMIE OLIVER'S ARMY
Steph, who cannot bear unresolved issues and considers herself to be a born organiser, asks who would like a piece, and then takes pizza cutter and divides slice (lengthways, so everyone gets some crust and topping) into several very thin strips.

THE CAN-DO!S
Phil tackles the situation head on by asking, "Who will share this last slice with me?" Invariably no more than one person will – so Phil simply subdivides the slice. Simples.

WHITE VAIN MAN AND NO SUGAR BABE
Louise eats only one slice of (no cheese) pizza anyway, and Jamie keeps it to two. As renouncing pizza reminds him of his powers of self-denial, he will force any polite slice on guests.

THE JACK PACK
Using their keen interest in fast-food psychology, Mark or Sophie asks if anyone wants the last slice, knowing everyone will decline – then takes it, implying that s/he has done everyone a favour by eating it.

THE ALT.MIDDLES
Caught between a) loathing of excessive politeness and b) their own good manners, the alt.middle stares glumly at pizza and becomes depressed.

THE DAMN-WRIGHTS

Jeremy and Carol ("Jez" is fine for friends, but Carol is definitely *not* Caz; she thinks it sounds like "a bloody chav name") work in business – Jez for the UK sales division of a German food-processing equipment manufacturer, Carol as a manager in a media-sales company. Educated at local state schools that they claim were rougher than they really were, they are now in middle age with two kids, Jack and Francesca, in primary school. They live in the first village you come to after crossing the ring road of their Midlands city, but they never name the city as their home because they are proud of being "rural".

What people notice most about meeting Jeremy and Carol for the first time is their anger. They seem to be angry about *everything*. Politicians. The police. Bankers. Chavs. Speed cameras. Premiership footballers. Call centres. Eco-prats who whine about cars (Jeremy has a beloved Subaru Impreza, Carol uses the VW Sharan). Modern pop music (they believe it has been going downhill since 1988). Most things on television (Acceptable: *Top Gear* and *Loose Women*). Did we mention politicians?

Carol 1 Sat Nav 0

The truth is that Jeremy and Carol always were a bit grumpy, but their dislike of political correctness, Labour's nanny state, the bank bailout, and then the MPs' expenses scandal, made them more political. Now, feeling ignored and equally angry at both the "benefits class" and the bankers, both of whom seem to be prospering at their expense, Jez and Carol are stormtroopers of the first group for many years to be aggressively, even militantly, middle class. They openly admit they want to live as far away as possible from the poor and working classes, but they are also scathing about the nepotism and vague crookedness of the super-rich. They loathe both old- and new-money establishments, and have no time for the old-fashioned snoots who run things in their area. As for Cameron and Clegg, well they might be an

ACCORDING TO JEREMY, PEOPLE DON'T REALISE

Climate change has happened before

The Queen is now actually subject to EU law

Most of the Labour Party were Communists

Aids isn't actually caused by a virus

Women and men are biologically different

Every shop assistant is empowered to knock up to 50% off the price of anything

Gareth in *The Office* was actually right about a lot of things

Britain is bankrupt

In 10 years' time white people will be in the minority in Britain

Milton Keynes is actually really nice, and a top night out

Did he mention Britain is bankrupt?

Don't get Jeremy started

improvement on Brown, but Jez and Carol are still unconvinced. Ideally they'd like Maggie back.

In many ways the restless Damn-Wrights are more comfortable travelling than doing anything else. They don't exactly *like* functional, on-the-move environments such as airports, business parks and service stations but they are at ease with them. For work and leisure, they tend to travel away from the city centre rather than into it; they both have an immense knowledge of the motorway system, which they secretly like to pit against their full-spec sat navs, anticipating where they might misread the road.

Work is important to them, and it draws out strong emotions. Convinced that Britain has millions of scroungers who choose not to work at all, Jeremy and Carol profess annoyance at the long hours they

SPIRITUAL LEADER

BANDS JEREMY AND CAROL WOULD GO TO SEE

Jeremy and Carol love going to see bands from
their youth. Their favourites include:

- U2 (though Bono "should give it a rest")
- Genesis (post Peter Gabriel)
- Dire Straits
- Simple Minds
- Queen
- The Who
- Jools Holland
- Take That (Carol only!!!)

Queen are actually better without Freddie

have to do themselves, although friends think they
seem to enjoy "slaving away". They certainly enjoy
the equipment. Both, for example, have the best in-
car phone speakers you can buy. Both secretly love it
when they have a passenger, and they talk to someone
else in another car in a three-way conversation; it
makes them feel like a good host, although in reality
the passenger and the other person tend to be aware
of each other feeling slightly awkward.

Away from work, visiting retail parks or holiday
centres perhaps, their personal style has the curious
quality of belonging to no definable period. Jeremy
likes light-blue jeans (worn quite tight, a 1980s
hangover), leather jacket, suede shoes, and keeps
a pair of Merrell trainers in the boot with his golf
clubs. Carol is well groomed, blonde and favours
tight, bootcut jeans, pointy boots and an outsize
chunky cardigan rather than a coat. For holidays
they'll get some new bits at M&S, Jez always being
impressed by the value for money offered by the Blue
Harbour range.

They love their holidays, because almost every

PLACES JEREMY AND CAROL DON'T GO TO ANY MORE

Ruined by idiots

Overrun by chavs

Too many screeching kids

Taken over by people
you want to kill

Full of students

Hosts annual international
moron convention, seemingly

THE NEWS: IT JUST GETS WORSE AND WORSE

Jeremy and Carol enjoy the news because it makes them so angry. Each story on each bulletin makes them progressively more furious and friends consider it likely that one day, one of them will actually explode. "At least we could sue to get the licence fee back if we did," jokes Carol.

BLOOD PRESSURE

BONG!

BONG!

BONG!

BONG!

BONG!

BONG!

6) PUBLIC ART PROJECT INVOLVING WEE, TURN IT OFF BEFORE I COMBUST!

5) BANK BOSS GETS TRILLION DOLLAR BONUS OR SOMETHING

4) MIDDLE-CLASSES LOSING OUT AGAIN

3) SOMETHING ABOUT HEALTH AND SAFETY, CAN'T EVEN UNDERSTAND IT

2) FRENCH SENDING MIGRANTS TO BRITAIN, FFS!

1) STRIKE - CAROL HAS TO CANCEL MEETING

NEWS HEADLINES

THE FACEBOOK FREEDOM FIGHTER

Jeremy Damn-Wright I love the smell of burning GATSOs in the morning!

BURNING GATSO!!!
www.youtube.com

🎞 Tues at 20:31 · Comment · Like · Share

Jeremy and Carol joined Friends Reunited a few years ago to see what had happened to the people they were at school with, but after that they did not bother much with social networking. In fact until recently they were not overly excited by the internet in any form, regarding it as a nerdy substitute for face-to-face conversation. What changed things was Jeremy's discovery that you could embed YouTube videos in your Facebook page – he now competes with friends to find ever-funnier footage of vandalised GATSOs and people having painful accidents. Carol joined at the same time, but used it mostly to play Farmville (which she has now given up) and bitch about contestants on TV talent shows. Both of them are increasingly annoyed by receiving endless requests to join groups.

country in the world (except France) seems to them more sorted out than bloody Britain – although the Brits are good at ruining anywhere of course. The Damn-Wrights used to holiday in Florida but like other places they used to go, it got spoiled when "every idiot with a passport" started going. Now they prefer Portugal or Phuket, where Jez will relax with a Lee Child and Carol will annoy herself with her *Marie Claire*. They will also discuss how annoyed the teachers were when they took Jack and Francesca out of school in term time so the holiday would be cheaper. The Damn-Wrights think that most of the teachers are bloody useless; Jeremy reckons he could do a better job himself sometimes!

It is important to note that Jeremy and Carol do hold some "seriously different" attitudes. When

OH FOR CHRIST'S SAKE

DO-GOODER

Jamie Oliver

MESS

Amy Winehouse

UP HERSELF

Caroline Flint

NOT HER AGAIN

Kate Winslet

BORING BASTARD

Andy Murray

GOD HELP US

Rowan Williams

SWOTTY GIT

Daniel Radcliffe

SUCK MY EXHAUST PIPE

Al Gore

WELL THANK F**K FOR THAT

GENIUS

Jeremy Clarkson

FEISTY

Ann Widdecombe

BIG BOLLOCKS

Gordon Ramsay

TALKS SENSE

Duncan Bannatyne

UNDER VALUED

David Davies

BLOODY HILARIOUS

Arthur Smith

BRILLIANT MIND

Dan Brown

GOD

Jenson Button

The views expressed here are those of Jeremy Damn-Wright and not The Middle Class Handbook

THE DAMN-WRIGHTS SUB-TRIBES

PSYCHO YUPPIES

Fraser and Ruth. Live in contemporary gated riverside housing complex. In their twenties, employed by mid-sized corporation and equity company respectively, dedicated to work and highly aggressive in pursuit of material reward. High-street tastes but fans of what they call the "greed-is-good era"; may even wear 1980s clothes in tribute.
Role models: Ben Clarke & Ruth Badger from The Apprentice

THE NEW LARKINS

Adam and Phillipa. Live in Victorian terrace in provincial city, most commonly in the west country. Work for local authority and struggling small retail chains (wine). Feel bitter that intelligence and taste "being squeezed out", and that "being middle class is a disadvantage". Hate fashion/celebrity but grumblingly watch *The X Factor* and shop on the High Street.
Role models: Ian Hislop & Jo Brand

COWPUNKS

Simon and Nicky. Live in detached house in rural area. Works in sales for agri-chemical company/as part-time admin role for local hospital. Previously conservative and non-political, found frustrations galvanised by campaign against the hunting bill; have only become angrier. Work in public sector increases irritation at "chucking money away".
Role models: Ann Widdecombe & Nigel Farage

MATALAN'S DRAGONS

Ken and Barbara. Live in ex-local authority terrace in mid-size ex-manufacturing town. Ken is supervisor in car components factory, Barbara secretary in higher education college. Enjoy doing up house, gardening and going to Canary Islands. Former traditional Labour voters, patriotic, proud of never claiming benefits; feel assailed on all sides, particularly by new immigrants and underclass.
Role models: Few, but susceptible to unexpected nostalgia for Mrs Thatcher

it comes to politics, for example, Carol tends to be more vituperative and blames individuals, while Jeremy shakes his head and blames the Government. They bicker about each other's personal faults, often publicly and entertainingly when they've have two bottles of the excellent Chardonnay they buy from the wine club. This is the only trouble with them as a couple, say their friends. They're good company, in fact they can be quite charming (Jeremy knows this, and thinks he is a good flirt) but they can get a bit aggressive when they go off on their rants.

Feeling they are likely to be done over at every turn, Jeremy and Carol are increasingly happy to turn this aggression on people who cross them. They often have it in for shop assistants, who tend to annoy them with their aloofness. Jez and Carol love telling visitors how much of a discount they got off all their white goods, although their very close friends know the story behind this is not always as rational as they make out. The reason they have such a huge fridge, for instance, is that Jez thought the assistant thought he couldn't afford it. Actually they were dithering over the purchase because Carol correctly thought it was too big to look nice in the kitchen.

Where many middle-class people worry about appearing decent to other people, Jez and Carol want less to do with "society", particularly the welfare state. "Go on," says Carol, "explain to me why I should pay tax for someone who *chooses* not to work?" They tend to think they are the first people to have thought of the point, and have a habit of saying, "What people don't realise is…" when actually, the newspapers have been telling people about the relevant fact for weeks. All this annoys liberals ("Good!") but then, as Jeremy points out, the liberals are not queuing up to pay more tax either. It might be easy to criticise the Damn-Wrights, but they are not, at least, hypocrites.

WINE: WHAT WILL THE NEIGHBOURS THINK?

"Knowing a bit about wine" is a hallmark of modern middle classdom, but it brings modern problems. A key dilemma: which bottles do you keep for yourself, and which do you take when visiting friends?

THE LIBERAL ACTUALLYS
Home: Grosset Watervale Riesling, bought from friend's new online wine business.
Away: Depends if host knows much about wine. If so: Penfolds Shiraz Cabernet. If not, opportunity to offload M&S Pinot Grigio received as Christmas gift from Emily's dreadful admin assistant.

WHITE VAIN MAN AND NO SUGAR BABE
Home: Il Cortigiano Prosecco.
Away: Oyster Bay Marlborough Sauvignon Blanc, Veuve Clicquot for special occasions.

THE DAMN-WRIGHTS
Home: Case of Bric Corderi Barbera d'Asti Superiore and Mâcon-Lugny 08 Louis Latour Chardonnay every six months from the *Sunday Times* wine club.
Away: Exactly the bloody same, why?

THE CHAVEAU RICHES
Home: Classic Bordeaux, a recent replacement for Châteauneuf-du-Pape, which hasn't been the same since that snobby twat laughed at Scott's pronunciation of it.
Away: Piper-Heidsieck ("Just f***ing call it 'Piper', Scott").

THE FAIR TO MIDDLINGS
Home: Campo Viejo Rioja (on offer in Tesco).
Away: Knock on Wood Sauvignon Blanc from M&S (Sylvia loves the label!).

THE CAN-DO!S

Home: Constant experimentation; rarely drink same brand more than twice.

Away: Wolf Blass Yellow Label Cabernet Sauvignon. Yellow is "amazing branding".

THE JACK PACK

Home: Blossom Hill White Zinfandel Rosé ("Sounds so lovely!").

Away: To impress, Canaletto Pinot Grigio; for parties, the cheapest non-supermarket own-brand bottle, own-brands being "chavvy".

THE ALT.MIDDLES

Home: Dr. Loosen Riesling from Oddbins (which they still visit out of loyalty despite all the changes).

Away: St Hallett Gamekeeper's Reserve.

JAMIE OLIVER'S ARMY

Home: South American Malbec from Naked Wines.

Away: Kumala Western Cape Pinotage Shiraz (looks a bit unusual and dearer than it actually is).

THE LOFT WINGERS

Home: Any Sainsbury's own-brand – unpretentious yet reassuring.

Away: Georges Duboeuf Beaujolais, a tip-off from Tom's dad, who knows A LOT about wines.

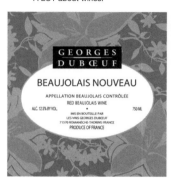

THE HORNBY SET

Home: Averys French Country White 'Terret-Viognier'. Secretly unable to find an organic wine they really like.

Away: Yalumba Barossa Organic Shiraz.

THE CAN-DO!S

Phil and Sue Can-Do! are really positive people, and dedicate their lives to, as they like to say, thinking out of the box. Both divorced from partners they married too young, they are in their late thirties and seriously impressing their friends with how well their business is doing.

Actually, let's be a bit more accurate about that "impressing". With their business LiveGood!, Phil and Sue are prompting, in most of their friends outside the HR training industry, feelings of amazement and even bewildered jealousy. Who would have thought, when they were entertaining guests at a party yet again with yet another corporate-psychology role-playing game, that they would even make a living out of this stuff? Anyone who imagined they would make enough to employ two staff and have had their garden redesigned as a "living thought-space" would have been mad.

OK, as the Can-Do!s might say – let's do some background. Both Phil and Sue previously worked in marketing but about 10 years ago decided to change their lives with self-improvement classes. That led to

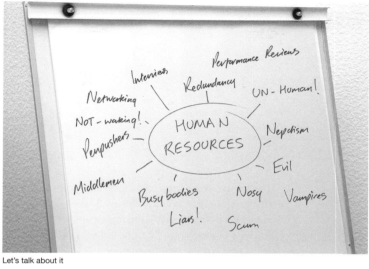

Let's talk about it

an interest in training at work, and before they knew it, they were running their own small "enabling" business, LiveGood!

LiveGood! "is geared to improving inclusion, increasing input, and developing empowerment and ideas-flow in the workplace by introducing counter-intuitive creative thinking and processes". It improves and enhances all the intangible assets you can't put on a balance sheet, like idea-fertility and communication flow. Its basic product is Phil and Sue's "adventure days", during which they use various exercises and role-playing to encourage managerial staff in large corporations to think creatively and improve their working relationships. Often the staff are cynical ("inhibited", says Phil) but senior managers enjoy it, and keep re-employing them.

THE CAN-DO!S LOVE	THE CAN-DO!S HATE
♥ Malcolm Gladwell ♥ Carole Caplin ♥ Phil Brown ♥ Alvin Hall ♥ Trisha Goddard ♥ James Caan ♥ Gok Wan ♥ Lifehacker ♥ Neil and Laura Westwood, the Magic Whiteboard™ entrepreneurs from *Dragons' Den*	✗ No one. Hate is a negative energy

And, although some old friends are sceptical too, Phil and Sue have many admirers. Deborah, who changed her life by retraining as a masseuse (she met Sue on a course called "Lateral Success"), thinks they are "21st-century revolutionaries".

Perhaps because they are so interested in crossing the "frontiers of the future" in their mind, Phil and Sue's radical thinking is not reflected in their home, which is a four-bedroom detached property in a commuter-satellite town 30-minute train ride from a conurbation. It has a hi-tech kitchen, but elsewhere the interior is strangely messy for people who have several acronyms to help people keep spaces organised – an easy one is FREE UP!

File paper
Remove anything you don't need
Engage immediately with incoming matter and
End your engagement with it in one go.

U are important, so remember to keep
Perspective!

MINDSCAPING BY THE FRIDGE

The Can-Do!s really like compound words such as Freeview, Wellman and liveright because they sound so contemporary and dynamic. When inventing their own, they often add some lively punctuation, too (Can-Do!s don't like to be limited by conventional grammar – hence the interestingly-positioned exclamation mark in their name). To help think of a name for their company, they made some fridge magnets and tried out various combinations using one word from each column; what do you think they chose?

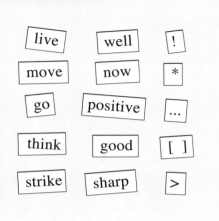

Sorry, as Phil would say, just a little ideas overflow there – back to the house. The furniture is mismatched, with ergonomic chairs, and a few pieces from the more expensive IKEA ranges; neither Phil nor Sue can be bothered obsessing over interior design (they love the bit in *American Beauty* where Annette Bening worries about the beer spilling on the couch – it says so much), and believe homes should be "living machines". The kids like this; it's one reason why they seem so relaxed.

The kids situation is complicated, with Sue's daughter, Gabe, living at the house but Zack and Megan, Phil's children, only visiting at weekends and holidays. Phil and Sue, however, feel this works. They have talk-sessions every so often, in a special "crash-pad" area of the kitchen where everyone can

TOOLS OF THE TRADE

Phil and, to a lesser extent, Sue are passionate about gadgets and stationery that help them achieve optimum performance. They keep keen eyes open for any new equipment, ostensibly for practical reasons but also because they just really like *stuff*. In fact, they sometimes wish they needed more heavyweight stuff like the iPad, as tools somehow lend them an air of substance. Essential kit for 2010 includes:

1	Keyfinder	8	Name badges
2	Bean bags (for bag-toss icebreaker)	9	Several corporate memory sticks
3	Blu Tack	10	Plantronics Voyager 520 Bluetooth headset
4	iPad	11	Whiteboard
5	iPhone	12	A variety of pens and markers
6	Laser pointer	13	Post-it notes (various sizes)
7	Mints		

GOOD!

Circles
Beanbags
Horizontal
Questioning
Comic Sans
Open palms
Taking ownership
Exploration

BAD

Squares
Desks
Vertical
Complaining
Times Roman
Pointing fingers
Passivity
The need for "results"

raise issues. Now the kids are approaching puberty they are beginning to find these excruciating, so invent problems in order to avoid the embarrassment of long silences.

Phil's son does find dad's work quite interesting, though this is partly because of the brilliant gadgets he uses. Phil and, to a slightly lesser extent, Sue are very keen on things they can use for training, and have boxes of the stuff. Much of this isn't really needed, but both secretly wish they did a job that needed more tools (see opposite). It was this wish that led Phil to adopt his Bluetooth headset. He also has an impressive set of Japanese kitchen knives, and loves the technocracy of the Audi A4 (Sue has a Citroen C3 Pluriel.)

Outside work, they love travel – they've just been to Central America for the third time (the islands off the coast of Panama, amazing), and are going to Laos at Christmas. They're also interested in Turkmenistan, Kazakhstan, and maybe even Iran, though right now might not be such a good idea! They bring back stuff that they use in training

BUSINESSES THEY WOULD LOVE TO PITCH TO THE DRAGONS' DEN

WHO MOVED MY CHEESE BOARD?
Branded range of kitchenware.

THE KEEPTRACK RACK
A simple, small cabinet-like storage unit that holds up to 50 USB memory sticks of varying shapes and sizes. Phil and Sue own more than 50 of these between them, and know what a nightmare it is trying to keep track.

LIQUIDTHINKING
Idea-capture system for recording thoughts and ideas discussed in "water-cooler moments" and then promptly forgotten.

THERE'S NUDGE PLACE LIKE HOME
System of tools and gadgets using ideas taken from Richard H Thaler and Cass R Sunstein's book *Nudge: Improving Decisions about Health, Wealth and Happiness*, but adapted for use in the home. Would begin with fly stickers along the lines of those used on the urinals of Amsterdam's Schiphol airport.

MINDRETREAT
A Center Parcs-like complex functioning as an ideas-sharing centre for people interested in personal development and training.

The Can-Do!s bring really interesting things back from holiday

to show how different objects can be perceived differently by people. When not travelling, they try to pick up new skills, and when not picking up new skills they devour non-fiction books; thoughtful, psychology-based stuff for Sue, and motivational thinking for Phil.

Clothes are not always a great giveaway because the Can-Do!s are not style conscious, but they are distinguished by a penchant for classics just outside of the trend cycle; Phil likes gingham shirts, moleskin and hiking shoes, while Sue often wears crew-neck sweaters from UNIQLO and Joseph trousers. They are far more interested in communication technology. As well as loving their iPhones ("if you're not getting your news on your mobile," they tell clients, "you're getting 'olds'!"), they have hundreds

SOCIAL NETWORKING WITH PHIL AND SUE

LinkedIn Network Updates   Dec 8 - Dec 15

FEATURED UPDATES   See more updates »

PROFILE

Phil Can-Do! has updated their current title to Business Coaching Consultant at
Think Positive! Send congratulations »
Sue Can-Do! has an updated profile *(Expertise)*

 STATUS

Sue Can-Do! has a new Icebreaker she wants to try Add a comment »

 GROUPS

Phil Can-Do! has joined Think Positive! Slough Empowerment Day!
Sue Can-Do! has joined Free Tibet With Positive Thought

APPLICATIONS

Phil Can-Do! is now using LinkedIn for iPhone. Learn more »

Phil and Sue make the most of LinkedIn, and find it invaluable for keeping up with contacts. They have hundreds of friends on Facebook, though they are usually too busy blogging to update their status. They have really been going for it on Twitter recently, and follow more than a 1000 people between them. Sue thinks Stephen Fry is amazing.

of friends on Facebook, keep a well-updated though little-read blog on their website, make the most of LinkedIn, and really love Twitter, each of them following hundreds of people. Friends are surprised to note that, despite this welter of information at their fingertips, both Phil and Sue will be inexplicably uninterested in the new events that everyone else is taking in, until they see an online discussion about it a few days later. When Megan once challenged his ignorance, Phil explained there is an American theorist who talks about modal frames of network

THE CAN-DO!S SUB-TRIBES

YO! TEAM

Tim and Debs. Live within an hour of city centre in large, quirky home, e.g self-designed eco-friendly subterranean pad or houseboat. Have enjoyed great success with a business venture in retail/leisure sector. Use unconventional management practices, and are fond of business catchphrases. ("There may be a gap in the market – but is there a market in the gap?") Friends unable to believe their success.
Role models: Simon Woodroffe & Oprah

FARROW & BORED

Tomas and Ayesha. Found equally in towns, and cities, and to a lesser extent villages, typically in medium-sized, tastefully decorated flats. Mildly bored with solid career in business, they now apply their drive to self-improvement projects, particularly those benefiting body, mind and spirit. Tempted by "more creative" careers.
Role models: Brian Cox & Stella McCartney

EMPOWER GENERATION

Paul and Oyinda. Live in flat close to the centre of their community, which may be town, village or city, and work most commonly in public or charity sectors. Use considerable social skills to bring people together and instill sense of purpose; prefer small communities to solutions from state politicians. May previously have worked in business.
Role models: Barack & Michelle Obama

SMALLTOWN HUBSTERS

John and Jo. Live in terrace in provincial market town, work in local shops. Keen participants in local community life, and love organising anything from local support-our-troops music nights to protests against new supermarkets. Never political in a party sense, are using technology for a new form of activism. Love Facebook; friends secretly wish they wouldn't invite them to join so many groups.
Role models: Jon Morter & Joanna Lumley

information. "God, Dad!" she said, "I was only talking about Girls Aloud."

Phil and Sue are part of a generation of people who in the 1990s embraced new ways of thinking about work and business, essentially combining both New-Age ideas that had emerged in alternative culture in the 1970s and 1980s with thinking from psychology. They find in each other the same interest in new ideas, and the same conviction that they can, in their small way, change the world. There is something evangelical and religious about their world view, perhaps because it depends on changing the external world by changing individual outlook and personality. Their generation has explored those ideas in myriad ways, but for those in business, like Phil and Sue, all this feels deep – a way of rolling work, lifestyle, personality and leisure together. When they talk about consumers and work and business, they feel they are talking at one remove about the fundamental truths of human nature.

It is true that many people dislike this idea, and are quite happy to retain what the Can-Do!s call "compartmentalisation", and equally true that their approach to work is sometimes ridiculed (the Can-Do!s get annoyed, for example, by "buzzword bingo" and Alec Baldwin in *30 Rock*) but the fact is, cuts or no cuts, much modern business loves "creative thinking" and sees it as a way forward, so the Can-Do!s are here to stay. They have brainstormed the future, and it works – and it's pretty good fun, too!

WHAT'S YOUR BAG FOR LIFE?

The middle classes' usage of bags for life is not as simple as the inventors might have imagined. Not only do people own a number of these bags, but they will chop and change them to suit the occasion. A trip to the farmers' market or into town? That will require the favourite one...

THE LIBERAL ACTUALLY
Everyday: Sainsbury's bag for life.
Favourite: Bag from Modbury, Britain's first plastic bag-free town.

THE HORNBY SET
Everyday: Waitrose bag for life.
Favourite: Greenpeace Little Green Bag.

THE DAMN-WRIGHTS
Everyday: Tesco "Big Green Bag" (Whatever!).
Favourite: Hammer and sickle bag (from zazzle.com bought for Jeremy as a joke by his 17-year-old left-wing nephew with whom he has political arguments, but of whom he is nevertheless very fond. "I used to think the same at your age!").

THE LOFT WINGERS
Everyday: Much-reused carrier bag from obscure dance music shop in Brooklyn.
Favourite: Synch Bag by Serena Galdo Maxi Disco, bought in New York.

THE FAIR TO MIDDLINGS
Everyday: Sainsbury pack-a-bag.
Favourite: Tesco bag for life (ladybird design).

THE CHAVEAU RICHES
Everyday: Vintage-look Union Jack tote bag.
Favourite: "Warning: Loves Kinky Sex" bag (bought for Tash as joke by Scott; Tash: "I'll use it, I ain't bothered: I DO love kinky sex!")

JAMIE OLIVER'S ARMY
Everyday: Sainsbury's 2007 "I'm Not A Plastic Bag" by Anya Hindmarch
Favourite: Cath Kidston reusable bag for Tesco.

WHITE VAIN MAN AND NO SUGAR BABE
Everyday: Bloomingdale's Medium Brown Bag.
Favourite: Sainsbury's 2007 "I'm Not A Plastic Bag" by Anya Hindmarch; now so out of date it's vintage.

THE CAN-DO!S
Everyday: Turtle bag.
Favourite: Bag with name of his/her suburb, designed as part of an initiative to boost local trade.

THE ALT.MIDDLES
Everyday: Co-operative bag for life.
Favourite: Spoof Anya Hindmarch bags reading "I'm Not A Smug Twat."

THE JACK PACK
Everyday: Standard Morrisons' plastic bag for life.
Favourite: M&S Twiggy tote bag.

THE JACK PACK

Mark and Sophie, 26-year-old insurance company underwriter and 25-year-old admin assistant respectively, are snobs and they don't care who knows it. In fact, they want everyone to know it. "I hate going on buses!" Sophie loudly declares on the odd occasions she has to catch one in town. "They smell!" "Let's have a laugh at the chavs!" said Mark when they went to Cancun last year – feeling safely superior because they were staying in a friend's parents' timeshare penthouse-style apartment rather than a hotel. It's all sort of tongue-in-cheek and yet not; they do consider themselves aspirational, and enjoy paying a bit extra in order to feel they're getting a better deal than the masses.

They co-own a flat, that they really stretched to buy, in a new-build block on the edge of a town, which itself is on the edge of a large conurbation. The block is really handy for the link road and the motorway, which allows them to commute to work in the cars (her: Vauxhall Corsa; him: Audi A3 bought at an auction) that they pay for on finance schemes. They drive a lot; another advantage of the block is

Fan-plastic

that it is five minutes from the town-edge retail park
with a Tesco, a Sports Direct, Nandos and multiplex
cinema, Frankie & Benny's, Pizza Hut, Pizza Express,
Chiquito and Ask. (Their parents say the park is
"soulless"; Mark and Sophie laugh, and say they don't
know what their mums and dads are talking about.)

Seriously into their logos and branding, they have
decorated the flat in a similar style to their friends,
i.e huge telly, (they watch a lot of TV, particularly
American dramas with intriguing lead characters
who tend to be called Jack) and IKEA furniture,
though they believe their choice and combination
of items to be wittily original (Sophie would like
to be an interior designer, but never gets round to
enrolling on a course). The décor is typical of Mark
and Sophie's taste, in that they feel most comfortable

HOW TO SPOT THE JACK PACK

- Expensive haircut
- Toned abs
- Gio-Goi jacket
- Lacoste (various items)
- Abercrombie & Fitch polo shirt
- Diesel trainers
- G-Star denim
- Fossil watch
- Shoes bought online from Next Directory or ASOS
- Karen Millen dress for special occasions
- Oasis for work
- Warehouse dress for the weekend
- H&M (for him and her)
- Coast bandeau dress
- White Adidas trainers on Saturdays
- Upbeat expression whenever possible

Adidas is well cool

with things that have an element of edginess and individualism, but which won't make them feel vulnerable to mockery. Their clothes, for example, tend to have that distinctive modern style of High Street Underground. They wear things that reference high style or alternative cultures rather than actually belonging to them (Mark's Gio-Goi rave T-shirts, Sophie's fabulous counterfeit handbags) and their favoured brands imitate fashion houses or genuine independent streetwear. Grooming will be similar to that of a Channel 4 presenter.

Unlike many other middle-class tribes, the Jack Pack are simply not all that bothered about authenticity. V Festival, for example, is fine – Glastonbury looks too difficult and too expensive, and with V, you can go clubbing in town afterwards. At weekends they'll sometimes hit the leisure park at weekends, but they also like a big night out in town, mainly going to large superclubs and chain-owned bars and pubs like Wetherspoon's and Revolution. Sophie likes All Bar One; Mark thinks it's "up itself". They'll often do separate bar crawls of their

MARK & SOPHIE'S HOME COMFORTS

- Always tidy and vacuumed five minutes ago
- Heating on if temperature drops below 10°C
- Extravagant lighting tracks
- Fitted neutral-coloured carpets and IKEA furniture chosen for comfort
- Manhattan-skyline photo hung in hallway
- Car parked in garage, or so as to be visible from living-room window

They'll go there for their honeymoon

favourite pubs with groups of their mates and then meet in their favourite club at the end of the night in order to share a taxi and a kebab. Sundays are spent recovering in front of the TV.

Mark and Sophie are often compelled to do things because they know other people who have (they first went to V because Sophie's sister and her friends had gone, and one of them ended up going for a snog in the VIP section with a touring member from Scouting for Girls). Secretly, they are often bored after 15 minutes of whatever it is, just as they are often bored with their purchases by the time they get home. They don't actually like the "thing", so much as the kudos that partaking in that "thing" will confer. This is why they and their friends are constantly updating their Facebook status. It is quite possible that "Sophie is about to walk down the aisle" could appear on her page on her wedding day.

They do enjoy special experiences that indulge their elitist fantasies though; Sophie likes to make a big show of being a snooty, materialistic, luxe-obsessed fashionista princess, and Mark entertains the

MARK'S TOP T-SHIRTS

I'M WITH THE BAND

Wore it to V

Gio-Goi
it is what it is

Wore it in Ibiza

MIKE RIGA 08
Alu, ludzu!

Speaks for itself *

Home again

same wealth-as-fantasy scenarios, though for him it's a bit less individually aggressive. Sophie would like to be Mariah Carey; Mark would like to be in the Rat Pack, or one of those guy-gang movies set in Vegas. Mark loves Vegas – it is his favourite place, and he's been twice – and in some ways the popularity of the new Vegas during their youth tells you a lot about the culture that influenced them. A theme-park world dedicated to high-rolling and the idea of limitless, unworked-for cash; Las Vegas was in many ways a fantasy version of the United Kingdom in which the Jack Pack grew up.

Mark and Sophie came of age in boom-time Britain, studying (Mark studied business management, Sophie did tourism at a vocational university) and then entering the job market in the early Noughties when money and jobs were plentiful. In those days if you were willing to turn up for Uni and then do as you were told at work, you ended up with a good salary and seemingly solid prospects.

Times were good, and with no money worries, Mark and Sophie and their mates instinctively felt

* "Beer, please" in Latvian

WHAT MARK AND SOPHIE DID ON THEIR HOLIDAYS

When it comes to Mark and Sophie's summer hols, sun, sea, and sand are essential but the things that really count are the tanning potential, and what you can do at the resort.

It's true their holiday snaps look a bit samey – but that's because when Mark and Sophie are not tanning, they're doing activities. You don't take photos when you're on the jet-ski.

Cancun, Mexico

Kombo beach, The Gambia

Djerba, Tunisia

Corfu, Greece

Naama Bay, Egypt

Sarimsakli beach, Turkey

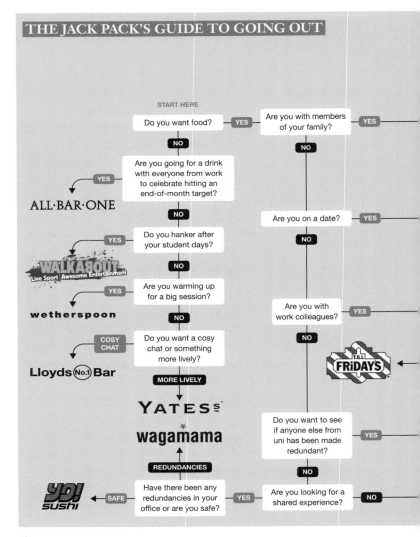

THE JACK PACK'S GUIDE TO GOING OUT

START HERE

Do you want food? — YES → Are you with members of your family? — YES

NO

Are you going for a drink with everyone from work to celebrate hitting an end-of-month target?
— YES → ALL·BAR·ONE

NO

Are you on a date? — YES

Do you hanker after your student days? — YES → WALKABOUT Live Sport Awesome Entertainment

NO

Are you warming up for a big session? — YES → wetherspoon

NO

Are you with work colleagues? — YES

Do you want a cosy chat or something more lively? — COSY CHAT → Lloyds No.1 Bar

NO

MORE LIVELY

T.G.I. FRiDAYS

YATES's

wagamama

Do you want to see if anyone else from uni has been made redundant? — YES

REDUNDANCIES

NO

YO! SUSHI ← SAFE — Have there been any redundancies in your office or are you safe? — YES → Are you looking for a shared experience? — NO

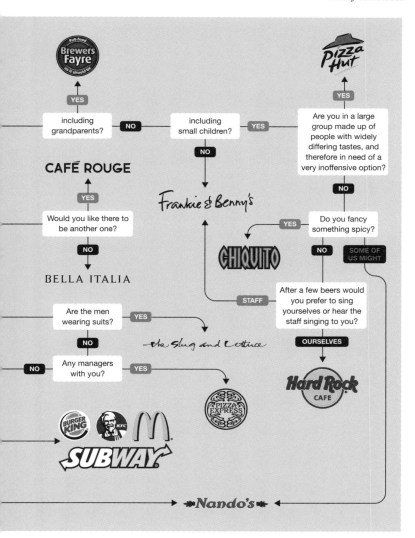

THAT'S BRILLIANT!

Lost
24
Glee

SNORE FEST

All cookery programmes
Most news programmes
QI

the most important thing was to seem happy and confident, and to appear as if you were on the up, successful and independent.

Sophie used to love dancing to Destiny's Child's *Independent Woman*, and it still reminds her of when she started working – the song summed it all up, really. In an age of easy credit, they spent and borrowed freely; switching credit cards and banks was a form of entertainment for them, a miniature version of the bankers' deals in the City.

It wasn't just about having money, but about having the feeling that having money was supposed to give you. True, they were never sure what that feeling was, but they acted as if they had it, assuming that that would make it come. This is why they didn't like to question whether luxury products and brands were really worth it (when Mark bought the +HD TV, he actually used the wrong cable for a month at first; he and Sophie still watched it insisting that it looked amazing). Even now, when declaring how happy and up for it they are, they sometimes seem to be in competition with each other. Ask how Mark is,

SOCIAL BICKERING WITH MARK AND SOPHIE

Mark Jack-Pack How come my birthday lasts one day but my other half's lasts a week?
6 hours ago · Comment · Like

 Pete Lyons Ha ha Know what u mean, Kate is still celebrating from last year lol
5 hours ago

 Mark Jack-Pack Seriously, how can u take three days off work for a birthday??? Women are mental. Fact.
5 hours ago

 Sophie Jack-Pack Mark thx 4 discussing my personal life with the world, will you please shut ur f***ing mouth
2 hours ago

 Mark Jack-Pack I'm not opening my mouth I'm typing lol, u only say thay cos u open your mouth to silently pronounce words when you read
1 hour ago

 Sophie Jack-Pack I cannot believe you, what about an apology? Twat.
1 hour ago

 Pete Lyons F***in hell guys – u know we can still see this right?
1 hour ago

 Sophie Jack-Pack Give me a minute, – I just need to change my relationship status
44 minutes ago

 Jo Cant Political views "Men are w***ers"!!!
41 minutes ago

 Sophie Jack-Pack I admit it I was wrong and have no sense of humour plus I smell
28 minutes ago

 Sophie Jack-Pack Oh Mark, so so hilarious, typing under my name when I go 4 a pee. Are you six years old? U really are a f***ing w***er.
5 minutes ago

 Mark Jack-Pack At least I have a sense of humour.

Mark and Sophie have a stormy relationship, and tend to see their rows almost as a form of entertainment for themselves and their friends. As they are also heavy users of Facebook, it was inevitable that their bickering would spill into cyberspace. Many of their friends have had their relationship etiquette complicated by social networking (stalker ex-partners being the most common problem); Mark and Sophie's problems are a relatively amusing example.

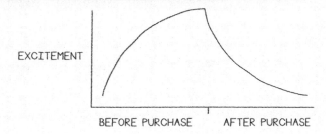

THE JACK PACK'S WAVE OF EXCITEMENT

EXCITEMENT

BEFORE PURCHASE   AFTER PURCHASE

and he'll say something like, "Topping, fella, topping, bang up for it tonight!" A bit like Vernon Kaye. Sophie likewise will not tell you she is "fine" but "really, really good".

In many ways, they *were* really, really good. Children of Blair, they were comfortable in their own country, and at ease when it came to issues that bothered some of their parents' generation. Their social circles included peers of various ethnicities; they didn't worry about jobs for life and security too much; they couldn't care less who was or was not gay or straight.

And yet, internally, this upbeat, finger-snapping happiness always masked an uncertainty as to what would actually constitute genuine contentment; they assumed it would be a decent car, nice holidays and good clothes, and when the car, holidays and clothes were not working, they assumed that they needed flashier and more expensive ones. It is easy to criticise this, but equally it is important to remember they were being told that the age of boom and bust was over, that shopping was a sort of patriotic duty,

THE JACK PACK SUB-TRIBES

CHUMMIES

Rob & Michelle. Live in new housing development in commuter town. Early 30s. Rob works in direct marketing, Michelle in travel company. Both have worked as travel reps. Have made careers out of being "outgoing"; fellow workers regard them as geniuses with persuasive e-mails. Friends say, "can be a bit… earnest".
Role models: Jake Humphrey & Fern Cotton

THE BRITTON EMPIRE

Phil and Sule. Live in period semi in commuter belt. Middle-aged middle managers for same same drinks company. Aspirational but proudly grounded; the human equivalents of a Ruth Watson hotel. Wary of seriousness, make a lot of jokes about sex. Everyone they have ever met says "A great laugh".
Role models: Meera Syal & Eamon Holmes

HOME RANGERS

Rana and Bina. Live in post-war semi-detached house in mid-size town; quality control manager and PA; independent and industrious, focused on family and friends rather than community. Semi-obsessed with house and keen on DIY; keen consumers, will debate difference between, say, Harveys and dfs sofas at great length.
Role models: Anjum Anand and James Caan

BORED FOCUS

Geoff and Una. Live in detached house in mid-income part of Milton Keynes with teenage kids. Spend more than half working life travelling; sometimes bored and thus very keen to feel plugged into major events.
General lack of role models but admire entrepreneurs, and joke about "Alan Partridge existence"

and that with ambition, the world was your Fine de Claire oyster.

However, in the past two years this thinking has been challenged by what is happening to friends who went to Uni and are still stuck in fast-food jobs. With no memories of the 1970s and 1980s, or even early 1990s, the idea of a recession feels as strange and puzzling as an alien invasion. Having assumed that the income and services would always be there, the Jack Pack are beginning to worry, and wonder if they might need to ask their equally hard-pressed mums and dads for a loan.

WHITE VAIN MAN & NO SUGAR BABE

In their early thirties, Jamie and Louise ("J" and "Lou") remain just as interested in shopping, fashion and looking good as they were in their twenties. In fact, despite their increasing age and the economic recession, they are if anything younger-looking and higher-spending than they were five years ago – a fact which owes something to the power of denial, and something else to Louise's new business interest – more of which later.

They have one son (Louise only wanted one), Rio, who is at a good state primary – they made sure the new house they moved to in 2007 (they made A MINT on their old three-bed semi, though the mortgage on the four-bed detached new build is a bit of a squeeze) was close enough to guarantee him a place. They were going to go private but decided against it – Louise didn't fancy competing with the stuck-up mothers, though they cut no ice with her. As she says, you don't get intimidated when you've booked them in for a wax, babes.

Jamie works with his dad, Trevor, in their commercial air-con business. It was booming until

Sunbeds are essential

a year or so ago – now they're just about scraping by, to be honest. Louise, meanwhile, is doing very well, making more than Jamie. A smart cookie with a beautician and nail bar in town, in 2006 she got someone to come in and do Botox. It went mad, and she launched her Bo-to Babes party service on the back of it. To cut a long story short, she now has new premises and offers a full range of surgical enhancements. Everyone says her people get a really natural effect. She's even done Jamie, though he doesn't tell anyone. Jamie's mum was very sceptical, but now she comes as well!

Louise and her friends have changed in the past five years, but it's not just having more money that has done it. Around the time *Sex in the City* was achieving critical mass on TV and *Grazia* was

JAMIE'D DO A JOB FOR...

| Quirky but cool | Dark but sexy | Great legs | Great everything |

LOU'D GIVE A FREE MASSAGE TO...

| Intriguing | Smart | Cool | That Italian |

launching, the girls like Lou, who wore Von Dutch caps and sexy slogan T-shirts, began to split into two camps. One group – many of whom became The Chaveau Riches (Page 121) – essentially took Jordan as a role model. The other – which included Lou – went upmarket following Victoria Beckham (a woman for whom Lou has profound respect).

The Beckham group abandoned hair extensions, and swapped designers such as Versace or D&G for Chanel and Mulberry. They cooled on the gym and took up Pilates, wearing Stella McCartney for Adidas gear. They took down their boob implants from an E to a C cup and covered their midriffs, but took to dressing up to the nines for even the most everyday occasions. ("Jeez babe, you're only going to Sainsbury's!" says J, but Lou is no fool. She loves

THE SECRET MEANINGS OF JAMIE AND LOUISE'S HAIRSTYLES

THE DEFENSIVE
Fashionable, but basis of classic bob means no one can accuse Lou of trying too hard

THE DEFIANT
Luxurious length says: I may be a mum, but I'm still in the game, baby

THE SURRENDER
She tried to kick straighteners, but sometimes when her hair's being super-difficult…

THE UNIVERSAL
Won't annoy his dad, still attracts comments from peers as a cut to be admired

THE STATEMENT
Says: I might be a dad, but I'm way cooler and confident than these novices in their twenties

THE PREMATURE MID-LIFE CRISIS
Jamie's proof that he's not too old to brush it forward

PARTY GAMES WITH LOU AND JAMIE

Identifying the cosmetic surgery that they think celebrities may or may not have had is all part of watching TV for Lou and her girlfriends. Sometimes after a few Proseccos, they plan to launch a new party game: *Spot The Work On The Celeb*. Jamie says Lou should do it, seriously – she'd make a mint!

Turkey Neck

Trout Pout

Pillow Face

Botox Eye

Droopy Mouth

Shrink-wrap cheek

AMANDA HOLDEN

JESSICA SIMPSON

GORDON RAMSAY

MADONNA

TERI HATCHER

TARA REID

It's Mojit-o'clock

Jamie and she knows he loves her and Rio, but men stray; look at her dad. You gotta keep 'em interested.) The Beckhamites can't quite renounce fake tan and sunbeds yet though. The true fashionista will have pale skin, but try as she might, Louise just can't give up the St Tropez.

In short, Louise, a turbo-charged consumer of the Noughties boom, is still shopping for England, but in a more consciously sophisticated way that allows her to look down on the more "obvious". (Cheryl Cole, by the way, spans both camps; she is pretty and nice enough for Louise, but Louise, with her new sophistication, knows Cheryl gives herself away a bit by still wearing hair extensions.)

Jamie and Louise's friends at The Queens (an old pub just outside the city centre, refitted in a

DIETS THAT LOUISE AND JAMIE HAVE TRIED

THE MAPLE SYRUP DIET
Made famous by Beyonce: 10 days consuming only a drink made from Madal Bal Natural Tree Syrup, lemon juice, water and cayenne pepper. Jamie lasted 36 hours.

THE SLACK-KINS DIET
A slack version of the Atkins diet: involves avoiding carbohydrate most of the time but eating junk on Sundays and allowing white wine. Their favourite.

JAMIE'S SPECIAL GYM DIET
Adapted from an article in *Men's Health*: chiefly involves bananas and protein bars. "Cheating!" said Lou, "You like those things!" "What about your cupcake thing?" said Jamie.

THE CUPCAKE FRIDAY DIET
Lou's invention: herbal tea for breakast, salads for all meals, but a cupcake binge with the girls on Friday. Cupcakes with pale icing favoured as they seem healthier.

HOW TO SPOT WHITE VAIN MAN

- Paul Smith suit, with slim lapels
- Omega Seamaster Chrono Diver watch
- Clothes tight and short
- UNIQLO pastel cashmere V–neck
- COS tapered cotton trousers
- Ed Hardy T-shirt
- Native American tattoo on shoulder
- Plimsolls
- H&M plaid shirt
- Lavish use of hair product
- Tight clothes to show off toned upper body
- Waxed upper chest
- Bloke-tox forehead
- Tie clip
- Striped T-shirt from Topman

HOW TO SPOT NO SUGAR BABE

- Chanel sunglasses
- Antonio Berardi
- 7 For All Mankind Jeans
- Louboutin shoes
- Mulberry bag
- Kate Moss for Top Shop seqinned dress
- Yves Saint Laurent purse
- Balenciaga Lariat bag
- Teeth veneers
- Tattoo of name in Mandarin on back, dove on wrist
- DVF dress from Net-A-Porter for weddings
- Jeggings
- Bobbi Brown and Chanel make-up
- Hair natural base colour but slightly enhanced

Can you tell?

Louboutins are classy

HOW JAMIE AND LOU HAVE FUN ONLINE

 Ford Force You need to get yoreself a fine lady, Barry my man, and "do what comes naturally!!!"
28 February at 15:56 · Comment · Like · See Wall-to-Wall

 Barry Doberry But how do I do that Ford, I dont meet any ladys when I am trainspotting at the station!
Yesterday at 19:39

 Ford Force Well Barry I can recommend to you a very fine lady of this town who works at a certain place called Assthetique, she is called Louise and very sexy, her husband is a total dork and I am sure she is ready for some away from home action!!
5 hours ago

 Louise No-Sugar-Babe Grow up Rajesh.
Yesterday at 19:39

Write a comment...

Both Jamie and Louise are seriously into their internet. Lou has a website for the shop (she got a few ideas from ASOS and Net-A-Porter, which she loves) and a Facebook account with loads of friends she has met through work. She socialises with lots of people she met as clients; like Lady Gaga's ex said, "All business is personal". One of the shop girls has started tweeting offers; Lou remains sceptical.

Jamie's big innovation is his Facebook alter-ego. Barry, who is a nerd, communicates mostly with Ford Force, a character created by Jamie's friend Rajesh, who is based on Austin Powers living in Guildford. Louise occasionally plays along, but she thought the joke stopped being funny ages ago. Still, that's Jamie – like a little kid sometimes!

minimalist style but still classically English and doing fantastic barbecues and mojitos in the summer) still say they're like the local Posh and Becks, though Jamie thinks Lou looks more like Cheryl Cole. He wouldn't fancy Victoria at all – far too skinny. Mentioning this at a certain point in the evening in The Queens can often lead to long discussions of everyone's sex lives; Jamie and Lou and their mates still consider it highly important to keep things interesting in the bedroom, and treat sex much like previous generations treated hobbies.

WHAT DOES JAMIE SEE IN HIS WATCHES?

1 THE BRAND

Watches are to Jamie what bags are to Lou, i.e they're expensive enough to still make a serious statement when everyone's got loadsaluxury goods. The brand shows your character – Omega's rugged, for instance, Breitling is a classic and TAG Heuer's cool. Jamie's a TAG man at heart.

2 THE BEZEL

Everybody loves the bezel, because it lets you get right into the technical detail when discussing a new watch. It shows you know your stuff. Lou says she doesn't believe he understands it all, cheeky mare!

3 OVERALL STYLING

All about the balance of sportiness and smooth sophistication. Jamie prefers sporty.

4 TIME ZONES

Jamie jokes he only uses them to tell him when World Cup games kick off!

5 FACE COLOUR

Colours are changing seasonally now, pressurising Jamie to keep up! But you have to love it though - it makes it all more interesting, doesn't it?

6 THE HANDS

All about the second-hand movement – smooth, or by the second? For Jamie, the latter – somehow it seems more precise, and it's all about the precision.

7 THE STRAP

Where you add the individuality. Leather for classic, metal for tough and sporty and rubber to be a bit out there. For Jamie it's got to be a nice metal link every time.

8 CHRONOGRAPH

Needs a nice crisp feel. Jamie uses it to time himself driving, though Lou's got her cheeky jokes about that!

LOUISE'S SENSE OF OCCASION

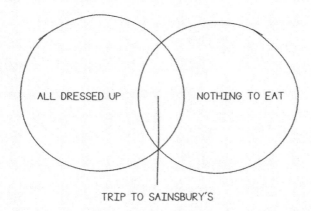

ALL DRESSED UP   NOTHING TO EAT

TRIP TO SAINSBURY'S

Jamie's fashion sense has gone in the opposite direction to Lou's in some ways. He's begun to follow younger men's lead in embracing the High Street and its disposable fashion (Topman, UNIQLO, H&M and, most of all, COS), which means he changes his look more often; sticking with Stan Smiths, dark jeans and Lacoste shirts is for his older brother, Adam. More important than the clothes, though, is his body; a devoted reader of *Men's Health*, Jamie takes diet and supplements seriously, and really enjoys going to his private gym (he knows the owner – him and his dad did the air con, so he's always sure of an extra-fluffy white towel, as he jokes).

Clothes and bod aside, of course, his pride and joy is still his car, these days a TVR Tuscan S. He's actually itching to change the TVR (Jamie hates

WHITE VAIN MAN & NO SUGAR BABE SUB-TRIBES

BRITAIN'S HOT TALENT
Joe and Shemani. Live with respective parents in affluent suburb of large satellite town. A-level students at local college, but describe selves as dancer and singer respectively. See life as pointless without fame; have achieved a degree of it already with local performances, and dress accordingly. Parents encourage sense of entitlement.
Role models: Diversity & Leona Lewis

25/8 GUY & GIRL
Max and Sadie. Live in city-centre loft space, but rarely there. Work in sales and marketing. Travel internationally for a third of the year, more familiar with, say, South Africa than their neighbouring county. Work constantly, frequently all night. Immense knowledge of airports. Friends complain of Blackberry use at dinner-party table.
Role models: Barack Obama & Carla Bruni

SECOND YOUTHERS
Graeme and Christine. Live in two-bed semi-detached house on modern housing development in village. Engineer at window company and social care worker. Began careers in manual work, have studied to progress to professional status; now in 50s, kids grown up, enjoying "second youth"; drink in style bars, bang into their gym – Graeme is a natural bodybuilder.
Role models: Darren Gough & Denise Welch

MACPACKERS
Stefan and Tyson. Live in expensive, rented city-centre flat. Management consultant and industrial designer. From Holland and Scotland originally, have lived in various European cities. Liberal politics, fashion-conscious, hedonistic, high-spending consumers. Have high turnover of friends.
Role models: Mark Zuckerberg & Jade Jagger

having cars for more than three years; he just thinks the shape starts to look old), and would quite fancy an Audi R8, though money's likely to be a bit too tight for that in the foreseeable. Lou, meanwhile, has swapped her Mini for a Discovery 4 – she doesn't do anything by halves. They thought about a Range Rover Sport, but decided they were becoming "a bit chavvy". It's important to be able to spot these things coming.

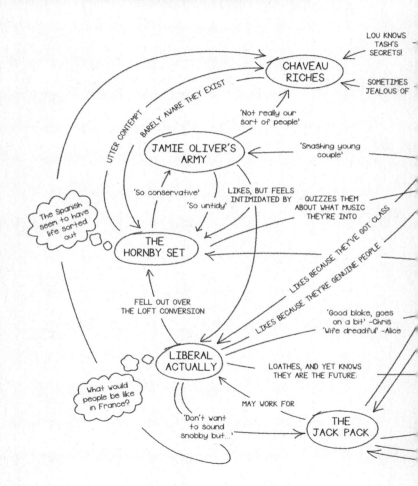

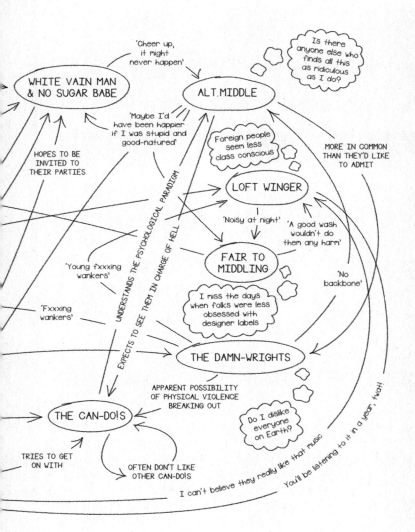

THE FAIR TO MIDDLINGS

Martin saw it coming

Martin and Sylvia have a joke about their lives these days – they haven't had a moment's rest since the day Martin retired! Of course they do relax, really (they still have proper sit-down coffee and tea breaks, with biscuits, in the morning and afternoon) and Martin, as a partner, still does a day or two a week in his old office (a chartered accountancy practice; he joined in 1975 as a 34-year-old). But their point is that they're involved in so many activities. Between doing the family trees on Ancestry, going to the U3A course meetings (they're doing social history), the am-dram, Sylvia's little volunteer job at Oxfam on the high street, *and* the cruises, it's absolutely non-stop!

Martin was very lucky with the timing of his pension; they think life seems much tougher for young people now than when they were their age, and they still feel an urge to help their offspring. In fact they have been putting away money for their grandchildren, Sara and Christopher, for some time – although this is a thorny issue because, of course, their daughter Felicity (36, known as Flick) and her partner Becky (they entered into a civil partnership

The cruise-ship shops were fantastic

last year, no family invited – Martin and Sylvia were secretly relieved) probably won't be having children, so is it fair? Martin says it'll all come out in the wash, but Sylvia worries.

Generally speaking, though, they try to keep up with things without being embarrassing about it, because they are caught between not wanting to be like their parents, who ossified aged 50, and fear of resembling those mutton-dressed-as-lamb chumps on some of these television programmes (they are still to this day reeling from the spectacle of Sly Stallone's mother on *Celebrity Big Brother*).

This desire to keep up and be involved is one reason why they remain involved with the local community. Because they had their names down as emergency planning volunteers, they spent last

FAIR TO MIDDLINGS DON'T LEAVE HOME WITHOUT

Martin

- Steel-rimmed specs
- Medium-width M&S cords
- Side-parting
- Shower-proof anorak for everyday use
- Nubuck leisure shoe (not for travelling)
- Cotton handkerchief

Sylvia

- Liberty silk scarf
- Max Factor pink lipstick
- Hand-sterilising gel
- Blue Husky jacket
- Sugarless peppermints
- Packet of wipes

A pair of binoculars can come in handy

Sylvia calls them pumps

winter ferrying old people around the snowbound streets in the Volvo! They secretly relish such adventures, combining as they do three of Martin and Sylvia's passions – community spirit, "challenges" and the weather; they are still telling guests about the last-minute dash to the vet's with Mrs Adamson's spaniel during the awful blizzard. Martin will illustrate the whole episode with cutlery and the cruet set if he senses you're really interested.

They are devoted to Radio 4 and Classic FM, but find themselves watching television less and less – although there are some good programmes on BBC4, Andrew Marr remains peerless, and they enjoy a lot of the gardening shows. Both of them have gone off the over-exposed Titchmarsh somewhat (they *do* miss Geoff Hamilton), but Sylvia is quite keen on Monty

WHO DO THE FAIR TO MIDDLINGS LIKE?

REALLY SMASHING

THEY'RE SPOILING IT

CAN'T BEAR THEM

Joanna Lumley (& Gurkhas)
Trevor McDonald
John Humphrys
Martin Clunes
Simon Cowell
Twiggy
Countryfile
Strictly Come Dancing
Gardeners' World
Rowan Williams
Ten O'Clock News
Holly Willoughby
Jonathan Ross
Politicians
Lady Gaga ("Aptly named!")
Piers Morgan

Don. She also likes Carol Klein (you don't often see a woman unafraid of getting her hands dirty on TV) while Martin is partial to Rachel de Thame (nothing to do with her looks at all!).

TV can be the source of much guilty pleasure for Martin and Sylvia – they occasionally end up engrossed by "tripe" on Channel 4 in spite of themselves, and are utterly unable to tear themselves away from *The Jeremy Kyle Show*. All their friends watch it, but feel it is so dreadful (why would anyone even want to *see* such things?) that the first person to bring it up in conversation always has to make an excuse ("It just happened to be on while I was making coffee"). They were especially appalled by the Jonathan Ross and Russell Brand debacle (Martin thinks Russell Brand is the same person as Johnny

HOW TO WIN A FIVER FROM MARTIN & SYLVIA

Over the years, the window in Martin and Sylvia's spare bedroom has become a standing joke. Guests have listened to Martin and Sylvia's instructions yet no one outside the family has ever been able to successfully open and – this is the clincher – close it. Martin and Sylvia see this as a source of amusement, and have offered a prize (£5) to the first visitors to do it.

1 Before you start to pull upwards just ease the window over to your right
2 Still pulling to the left, push upwards in one strong, firm movement
3 When closing, pull it down but also just gently tug it out away from the frame
4 And when it sticks at the bottom, just give it a gentle firm jerk downwards

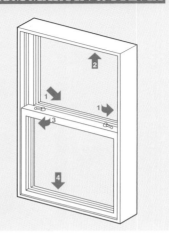

Which one is he?

Depp in *Pirates of the Caribbean*), and by the increase in scenes filmed in toilets in dramas. The sight of Julie Walters, playing Mo Mowlam, having a wee was a new low; how, Sylvia would like to know, was that essential to the plot in any way whatsoever? Shakespeare somehow managed without showing his characters on the loo, didn't he?

Repelled by TV, they resort to DVDs (period dramas for Sylvia, *The World at War* box set for Martin) and technology. They spend quite a lot of time on the internet, though mainly in the darker, more wintry months as they like to be out in the garden, or visiting friends, in the lighter evenings. They also have a webcam so they can talk to the grandchildren (Sara and Chris live in Switzerland now, having previously been in Hong Kong – their

SYLVIA'S GARDEN: ARRIVALS AND DEPARTURES

Hollyhock
Cottagea romanticus
Makes you think you're living
in the country

Chives
Herbivorum fashionabilista
Impressive when you snip them
into the new potatoes

Opium poppy
Talkingium pointis!
Endless jokes from Martin

Nasturtium
Chavis vulgaris
Some modern colours look so artificial

Dwarf Conifer
Historicus naffness
Flick took mickey out of them

SANDWICHES: THE FAIR-TO-MIDDLING CHOICE PARADOX

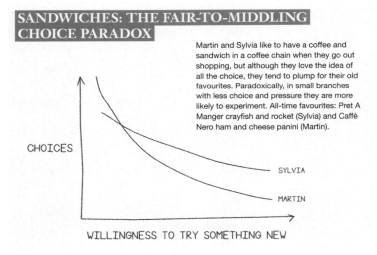

Martin and Sylvia like to have a coffee and sandwich in a coffee chain when they go out shopping, but although they love the idea of all the choice, they tend to plump for their old favourites. Paradoxically, in small branches with less choice and pressure they are more likely to experiment. All-time favourites: Pret A Manger crayfish and rocket (Sylvia) and Caffè Nero ham and cheese panini (Martin).

CHOICES

SYLVIA

MARTIN

WILLINGNESS TO TRY SOMETHING NEW

dad Jeremy is a hedge-fund analyst, and he, his wife Jenny and the kids, have to go where the work is), although they still feel self-conscious in front of it and the children get bored in 30 seconds.

The Fair to Middlings rather like new gadgets, not only because of what they can do but also because being able to use them competently is an unspoken form of one-upmanship among their peers. Both have mobile phones, and Sylvia was among the first of her friends to learn how to text (she bribed Sara to give her intensive lessons by buying her a pink iPod Nano; "Sylvia can text!!" was her first message to Martin). Truth be told, they are drawn strongly towards those gizmos which can be used to do almost exactly what an old one did (they insist that Classic FM on Freeview "sounds clearer", despite the sceptical

They blame themselves

looks from their children). When they come across digital versions of conventional, old-fashioned things, they snap them up like early adopters, although this often leaves them stuck with malfunctioning items that no one can sort out. They really liked the idea of the digital photoframe – it seemed a great idea for family photos and it can rotate them so no one gets offended! – but it soon started blinking and going negative, and the reset won't work. They both feel slightly at fault for not knowing how to get it working again.

Their big treat is travelling. Two years ago they tried a cruise – a risk, because while not wishing to appear snobbish, they had heard cruises could be somewhat vulgar – but they got a tip-off on one that had a more educational element, stopping off

THE FAIR TO MIDDLING SUB-TRIBES

SAGA LOUTS

Lionel and Jenny. Live in a detached house in wealthy suburb, 15-minutes' drive from Lionel's old business (fridge importing; his son runs it now). In late sixties and having best time of their lives, using generous pension plan to fund hedonistic pleasure befitting, as they see it, the wild Sixties generation. Snooty neighbours say "grow up"; they say "what for?"
Role models: Mick Jagger & Julie Christie.

THE CLASSICAL

Robert and Henrietta. Live in detached house in village; toy with idea of somewhere smaller but would miss garden. Retired professionals, possibly military/agricultural/ecclesiastical background. Proud adherents to classic English lifestyle, willing members of committees on which they have frequent run-ins with the younger set. Friends tell younger set, "they mean well".
Role models: Edward Fox & the Queen.

THE GRAN CANARIAT

Bernard and Angela. Live in generously-sized terraced home in outer suburbs. Bernard is recently retired after career as toolmaker, Angela keeps on little job at leisure centre. Aggressively respectable, lamenting number of "Jeremy Kyle kids" locally. Love Canary Islands, especially at Christmas,
Role models: Alex Ferguson & Helen Mirren

GREY GUEVARAS

Richard and John. Live in well-appointed townhouse in the conservation-quarter of cathedral town. Well into retirement after careers in academia and psychotherapy, they remain active and politically aware, leading local campaigns against luxury flat developments and speaking out against ageism. Friends, who they meet annually at the Hay festival, commiserate on how conservative Britain is.
Role models: Tony Benn & Joan Bakewell

at some sites of historical interest in the Med. It was really nice, just far enough – next time they'll go the other way and try the Fjords. They met some lovely people, and the change introduced them to lots of new things. They both developed a taste for Bombay Sapphire gin, which they hadn't tried before, and made a point of hunting down when they got home; that it was on sale in the local Sainsbury's didn't dull the lustre of exclusivity for them, as Martin and Sylvia tend to prize things according to when and where they discovered them, not where they're sold now. Hence Sylvia still thinks of the Olay brand as the most exclusive beauty product on the market (though she has switched from Oil of Olay to Regenerist 30 Second Wrinkle Filler cream), Martin thinks his old Swiss Army knife has a rarity value, and they both persist in believing Ferrero Rocher chocolates are "hard to track down".

Trying new things, travelling and learning; this is how Martin and Sylvia intend to keep living their lives. More than any other generation before them, they seek to avoid sounding like "old people", and avoid grumbling about music and fashion and the like. True, they do feel something has gone a bit wrong with our culture somewhere along the line, because the media and the law seem to celebrate the wrong sort of people, somehow. But these feelings have as much to do with their moral sense as with feelings of nostalgia, and they try to remain positive – almost competitively so sometimes. Upwards and onwards! As Martin likes to say.

THE SICK SOCIETY

It is an unwritten rule of modern British middle-class life that you cannot be simply "ill". Instead, one must have a self-diagnosed long-term "condition". Of course, there are many genuine sufferers like the people shown on these pages (they are regarded with a secret envy by the true new middle-class hypochondriac) but these days, each tribe also has it specific kinds of phantom illness...

JAMIE OLIVER'S ARMY
Used to be:
Annoyed by untidy kitchen
Now thinks might have:
Obsessive Compulsive Disorder

Genuine sufferer: Jessica Alba

WHITE VAIN MAN & NO SUGAR BABE
Used to be:
Bloated after meals
Now thinks might have:
Wheat intolerance

THE CAN-DO!S
Used to feel everyone was:
Uptight
Now thinks everyone is:
Suffering various forms of illness brought on by hyper-consumerist culture as described in *The Spirit Level*.

THE DAMN-WRIGHTS
Carol used to think Jeremy was:
Nerdy and obsessive
Now she thinks all men have:
Asperger's Syndrome

Genuine sufferer: Gary Numan

THE LIBERAL ACTUALLYS
Used to be:
Tired
Now thinks might have:
Seasonal Affective Disorder

THE CHAVEAU RICHES
Used to be:
Promiscuous
Now thinks might have:
Sex Addiction

THE HORNBY SET
Used to be:
Doing badly at school
Now thinks might have:
Dyslexia

Genuine sufferer: Keira Knightley

THE FAIR TO MIDDLINGS
Used to have:
A cold
Now thinks might have:
Exotic form of flu brought into country by mass migration

THE JACK PACK
Used to be:
Aggressive when drunk
Now thinks might have:
Bi-polarity

Genuine sufferer: Jean-Claude Van Damme

THE LOFT WINGERS
Used to be:
Hungover
Now thinks might have:
Food allergy

THE ALT.MIDDLES
Used to feel:
Depressed
Now thinks might be:
Clinically depressed

THE LOFT WINGERS

Tom and Anna have always insisted (somewhat falsely) that they are not concerned with being trendy, just with being "creative". In practice this meant working in the marketing departments of fashionable electronic-entertainment companies, while earning good money in their spare time organising events, publishing one-off magazines and selling their knowledge of emerging trends to friends at marketing agencies. Up to about 2008, this seemed like a job for life – well, until they hit 40 anyway.

Back then, they were confident that they would soon be moving from their flat in a Victorian terrace in their gentrifying working-class area to one of the cool new live-work loft spaces being created in the old warehouses down the road. Live-work lofts were something they aspired to, because such spaces felt like part of an anarcho-squatter heritage that, Tom and Anna felt, would link them to their leftist ideals even as they pursued what were really pure capitalist ambitions.

However, it didn't work out like that. By the end of 2008, the work on the side was drying up. The

Tom's bike is really fast

advertisers and sponsors pulled out of Tom's magazine, and the agencies and brands he consulted for became less concerned with aping trendiness than they were in the boom. In fact, to pay off credit-card debts, Tom has now had to take on some part-time work doing what is basically admin for a B2B newsletter organisation. He calls it, ironically, suffering for his art.

Accordingly, the flat, once full of new, modernist pieces from SCP and Skandium is beginning to look a little tatty. There are drink stains on the rug, the coffee maker has stopped working, and the vintage G-plan coffee table is still broken from when a friend fell on it during a mad party (they always have

AT HOME WITH TOM AND ANNA

Tom and Anna's current live-work space is a rented flat in a converted Victorian townhouse – a 15-minute cycle from the city centre. It has many functions – office, studio, living space and party venue – and a variety of décor, from collectable pieces to junk they have been meaning to get rid of for the past two years.

1 Bikes, hung on wall

2 Desk. With iMac. Always cluttered

3 IKEA Tylosand corner sofa unit in orange, bought secondhand off eBay

4 Vintage G-plan teak and glass coffee table Broken when someone fell on it at a party

5 Toshiba TV (not flat screen – it being a bit naff to care too much about your telly)

6 Immense stack of DVDs and CDs

7 Bric-a-brac arranged along window sills as ornaments. Includes: action figures; metallic-effect Buddha; wine bottle with candle; insects in Victorian cases (cracked)

8 Unwashed dishes

9 35 empty 330cl lager bottles for recycling

10 Decks (Technics, with 12" singles)

11 Bookshelves (IKEA Billy, full)

12 Walk-in wardrobe (crammed)

13 Three high piles of magazines; many other publications scattered across floor

14 Bed. John Lewis bedding that could do with a wash

15 A set of wooden antlers bought at their favourite Saturday market

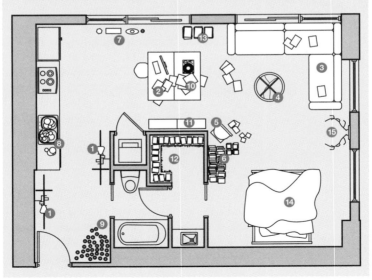

DRESS-UP PARTIES

Anna loves to host dress-up parties at her flat. Previous themes have included:

1 What's your favourite look for next season?
2 Alice gets shot in Wonderland
3 Trailer Trash vs. Sloane Rangers
4 Glee vs. Columbine
5 Poundshop party

WHO SHOT ALICE IN WONDERLAND?

JUNE 10 @SASHA593

STUFF THE LOFT WINGERS PROBABLY KNEW ABOUT BEFORE YOU DID

Tom and Anna pride themselves on keeping ahead of popular taste. They were over this lot before you'd even heard of them:

- *Flight of the Conchords*
- Bestival
- Smurfy Psycho
- The xx
- The National
- The nominations for this year's Mercury Prize
- *Scott Pilgrim vs. the World*
- *Misfits*
- Promoting events on MySpace
- Williamsburg

expensive broken things in their apartment).

Anna is faring slightly better, working for a small fashion PR agency (used to specialise in young designers; last two new accounts were a Littlewoods Christmas project and a relaunched search engine), and running her own club night, called "Trash Bitch". They play a mix of electro-pop, US 1980s power-pop and dubstep (actually, they say they play dubstep but play only one or two records a night – no one really likes it). Anna djs of course – she IS "Trash Bitch" and despite carting records to the warehouse venue every other Friday, she only ever "mixes" on her iPod.

The Loft Winger snobbery applies strongly to music. For example, Anna is a downloader, trawling through music blogs for all her new music but is

TODAY'S LOOK: ANNA

Eurotrash hooker meets 1950s burlesque dancer on a drug binge. Hair likely to be parted at the side, although if curly-haired may opt for an undercut.

- Washed-out T-shirts with deep V-necks are worn with stone-washed straight-cut jeans, turned up to expose brightly-coloured socks and second-hand brogues.

- Trench coat, probably from Aquascutum, worn for best while clumpy slip-on boots are worn over skinny trousers

- Basic T-shirts and tube dresses from American Apparel

- The occasional difficult-to-wear fashion piece

- Despite now rolling her eyes at the mention of said supermodel's name, Anna's look is a definite reincarnation of the one Kate Moss worked 10 years ago

- Red lipstick, the shortest and most cost-effective route to the avant-garde look.

Required reading

TODAY'S LOOK: TOM

Based on a combination of the hooligans he remembers from school, plus the 1980s Factory Records album sleeves. He's got a dandy-esque side-parting and, occasionally, a bit of a moustache.

- A pair of skinny jeans from Topman; has the same style in grey, blue and black

- A checked shirt in every check imaginable

- A worn-out waxed Barbour jacket. After deciding that the ones in the charity shop were too "smelly", he bought this one new, then beat it with a stick for a few hours

- White plimsolls bought from a market stall; also a pair of All Stars for every occasion

- Carries a worn-out copy of *The Ragged Trousered Philanthropists* everywhere with him – he even opened it once

- A worn-out herringbone Crombie or a leather jacket. Both were second-hand

Just required

PEOPLE THE LOFT WINGERS LIKE

Kode9
Charlotte Gainsbourg
The Smiths
Riz Ahmed

The Glee cast
Peter Andre
Martin "Wolfie" Adams
Coleen Rooney

Chloe Sevigny
Hot Chip
Burial
Fleetwood Mac

always careful to leave a selection of CDs and seven-inch singles strewn across the coffee table in case of unexpected visitors. Likewise her dress-up parties; thinking of a new theme will take her weeks. Likewise cycling. Bikes, which Tom protests are better and greener in every way than cars, are as important to him in terms of status as cars are to the Damn-Wrights (Page 36).

He loves to visit "the track" with his friends from "the (bike) scene", but does not think of this as having anything to do with status; he takes comfort in the knowledge that he is saving the Earth and is therefore much better than you. He gets around on his "fixy" (fixed-speed racer bike) and spends a lot of cash on the latest tyres (he frequently likes to swap colours), frame (vintage ones are his favourite) and lights. Tom is currently riding a 3Rensho, a bike his "friend" in the shop had imported from Japan; Anna is also a keen cyclist, and her bike is an old one Tom built from parts when he first got into riding – it's got a basket on the front now.

The Loft Wingers were always the only middle-

THE LOFT WINGERS ETIQUETTE GUIDE

ETIQUETTE

PUBS

Old-blokes' pubs rather than stylish bars should be sought out, as the former seem more "real". Likewise, pints of lager are more real than bottles. Getting very drunk is standard, as is loud advocacy of socialism and ironic discussion of crap TV. Bisexual behaviour while drunk is increasingly fashionable.

EATING AT HOME

Organic, free-range and generally healthy fare is desirable for wellbeing, but carry unwelcome connotations of bourgeois narcissism. A popular solution is to remove food from its packaging, and claim it is was bought from Iceland.

RESTAURANTS

A love of world cultures and personal earthiness can be communicated by eating in no-frills family-run Chinese restaurants. Ensure clientele is chiefly Chinese – and never, ever, eat in "Chinatown".

TAKEAWAY FOOD

Large donor kebabs from local kebab shop should be taken with extra chilli sauce, and then loudly described as "f***ing disgusting" before being left half-eaten. An alternative is home-delivered Domino's pizza, rendered ideal by its associations with American trash culture.

162

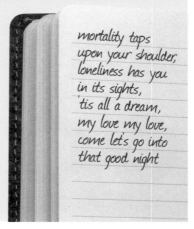

THINGS THAT LOFT WINGERS DO IN SECRET

1. Manipulate the most-played lists on their iTunes, adding plays to more credible artists

2. Spend 20 minutes writing and rewriting their Facebook/Twitter updates before posting them, in order to perfect the "natural" voice

3. Run the thesaurus over emails prior to sending, adding and changing words to create a more erudite/poetic tone

4. Listen to Elkie Brooks

5. Exorcise feelings of angst by scribbling in a little black Moleskine sketch book (if it's good enough for Pete Doherty...)

6. Sky Plus Jeremy Kyle

7. Watch romcoms starring Kate Hudson

*mortality taps
upon your shoulder,
loneliness has you
in its sights,
'tis all a dream,
my love my love,
come let's go into
that good night*

class group to be downwardly mobile, copying habits and clothes from the proper geezers and working-class girls in East London, and to an extent that still applies. However, there has been a slight shift. The white working class has lost something of its appeal (the BNP thing meant you could dismiss them as intolerant; secretly it meant you could stop feeling embarrassed about being better off) while sexuality and non-nationality are sources of the new credibility. They have little time for fellow Brits or Antipodeans – especially, in Anna's case, the attractive ones.

The large crowd among which you will find Anna when she is out is mostly young gay men who hail from the likes of countries such as Slovenia and Portugal. Tom, meanwhile, is "totally fine" with bisexuality, irrespective of who is in on the action. He

103

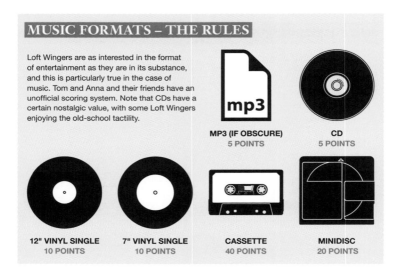

MUSIC FORMATS – THE RULES

Loft Wingers are as interested in the format of entertainment as they are in its substance, and this is particularly true in the case of music. Tom and Anna and their friends have an unofficial scoring system. Note that CDs have a certain nostalgic value, with some Loft Wingers enjoying the old-school tactility.

MP3 (IF OBSCURE)
5 POINTS

CD
5 POINTS

12" VINYL SINGLE
10 POINTS

7" VINYL SINGLE
10 POINTS

CASSETTE
40 POINTS

MINIDISC
20 POINTS

did in fact recently snog his best friend Alex while drunk; Anna thought it was quite cool. This attitude to sexuality is all part of a camp, draggy, Euro-trashy aesthetic, with its multiple levels of reference and irony functioning to exclude outsiders. This can be quite complex. For example, when a Loft Winger goes out for breakfast at a fashionable restaurant on Saturday (they like going out for breakfast on Saturday, not having gone to bed until 7am) they will sometimes archly say, "Let's catch brunch at a hip café in [insert name of their fashionable area]" to show they are self-aware. Should there be people in the café who have come from outside the area to look at the trendy people, Tom and Anna will sneer at them the way that, say, landowners in Wiltshire might sneer at chav tourists. In fact, the Loft

ANNA'S RULE OF CHARITY SHOP FASHION

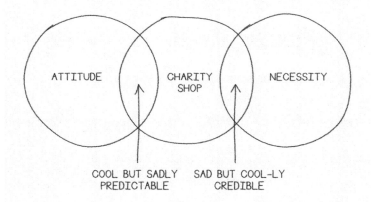

Wingers will refer to them as "chav tourists" or, more likely, "bridge and tunnel".

Still, while it is easy to knock the Loft Wingers, the fact remains that they're doing stuff and consuming new stuff that most of us might disdain now, but will be doing ourselves in two years' time. They are open to new ideas, and this is surely a Good Thing ("A God Thing", Tom says). As to what the future holds though – that is open to question. As a group they in many ways came of age in the 1990s, and they were the gatekeepers of new ideas in this period when Britain was going through a boom-time spasm of enthusiasm for the future and new ideas. In some ways they were the shock troops of New Labour; Oona King certainly knew a few of them.

In 2010, Britain seems to have had enough of the

SOCIAL NETWORKING WITH TOM AND ANNA

Danny and Anna use Twitter and Facebook almost every day. When Anna posts on Facebook and Twitter, she is likely to say where she is, and talk about her "super-talented" and artistic group of friends. Unless Danny is out drinking, he is more likely to share film clips or the music he is listening to. Trawling YouTube for, say, obscure old public information films and then posting them up for his friends to enjoy is a sort of social occasion in its own right for him.

Anna has a blog, mybeautifulworld.com – she says it is to document her musings on city life, but mostly it's her trying to be ironic. Her super-talented Slovenian friend provides the photography. Besides this, Anna also spends hours trawling music blogs for new music, especially on Fridays just after most of them have updated. And, finally, she promotes Trash Bitch with a Facebook group which Danny reckons is getting big enough for her to make money out of as a database or something.

THE LOFT WINGERS SUB-TRIBES

NOTTING PILLBILLYS

Alex & Lucy. Live in fashionable flat just outside city centre, and cottage in country. Supported by family money, run small businesses, typically in therapy or food sectors. Slavishly obsessed by new alternative lifestyle trends. "Make me feel guilty and stuck in the mud" say friends, "but then I don't have their money."
Role models: Hugh Fearnley-Whittingstall & Tamsin Omond

NEW YORK DALSTONS

Titus & Sascha. Rent scruffy warehouse conversion, dream of living in Brooklyn. Have fledgling (possibly stalling) careers in arts/media. Consumers of experimental art and fashion and, despite downwardly-mobile accents, are very competitive. Bisexual. Friends say they're "painfully trendy", they say, "creative".
Role models (this week): Yeasayer

MR & MRS CAN'T GIVE IT UP

Ben & Anita. Live in large, fashionably-furnished house in inner suburbs, work in media/retail/service industries, and despite middle-aged children are unable to relinquish youthful hunt for novelty and hedonism. Have an entire room full of LPs. Friends say, "Don't know how they do it", they say, "You only live once".
Role models: Brian Eno & Patti Smith

URBAN INFITTER

Tim & Samira. Rent in mid-suburbs/middle-sized towns, work in sales/service industries. Fairly conservative, but keen on brands and goods referencing "underground" culture without really being part of it; listen to "landfill indie" but don't call it that. Friends say, "cool", New York Dalstons say, "bridge and tunnel".
Role models: The Ting Tings & Scouting For Girls

future for a while; it is cosying up to tradition again. There seems a certain (multiple-layered) irony in the fact that when you see the Loft Wingers tucking into the pike and samphire or beef on the bone at Mark Hix, several of the older ones are likely to be wearing Barbours, Belstaffs, Tattersall shirts, shooting jackets, brogues and the like; country clothing associated with everything they detest. You could draw various meanings from this, but while it might be attractive for its authenticity, it doesn't really mean anything.

Perhaps that's the point. Superficiality was always the Loft Wingers' trouble. They didn't have beliefs, just a great sense of what looked right at the time. As it becomes harder to make money from that sort of thing, they may discover who they actually are.

THE SECRET MEANINGS OF CHERYL COLE

In modern Britain, being a true celebrity requires a persona that each sub-class can interpret to suit itself. Here's how it works for our newest national treasure.

THE FAIR TO MIDDLINGS
Well-mannered young lady to be admired for working herself out of poverty rather than complaining. At times a comforting reminder of former age.

THE DAMN-WRIGHTS
Relatively un-annoying celebrity, who at least works for a living and gives the impression of at least sometimes saying what she thinks. Also entertaining in her willingness to criticise other vacuous showbiz-types.

THE ALT.MIDDLES
Old-fashioned homegrown talent whose very manufactured-ness makes her vaguely reminiscent of girls from golden age of British pop.

JAMIE OLIVER'S ARMY
Good entertainer who you'd feel OK letting the kids watch. Kindness to the contestants on *The X Factor* is inspiring.

THE LIBERAL ACTUALLYS
Demure, nice girl who manages to combine decent manners and comportment with a modern, easy, relaxed classless air. Wish they could pull it off as well, frankly. Not sure about her taste in men though.

THE CHAVEAU RICHES
Brilliant businesswoman who knows how to make the most of what she's got. To be studied for lessons in taking opportunities.

THE LOFT WINGERS
Trash TV icon to be appreciated with ironic enthusiasm to convey anti-intellectual wit. Accent can be imitated when drunk.

THE HORNBY SET
Distinctive working-class voice amid bland mediocrity; showed courage in leaving Ashley Cole.

WHITE VAIN MAN & NO SUGAR BABE
Kindred spirit with an exemplary combination of down to earth-ness, aspiration and fortitude.

THE CAN DO!S
Great communicator who is to be admired and learned from for her instinctive and warm emotional intelligence.

THE JACK PACK
Amazing, almost life-as-soap-opera star who maintains interest by steadily and constantly moving on to new chapters in her life.

THE LIBERAL ACTUALLYS

Emily and Giles Liberal Actually are in their early forties, and live in a capacious semi-detached house in a tree-lined street on the outskirts of a major conurbation. And, before you ask, no, they still vote Conservative – the Liberal Actually thing is a nickname given to them by Giles's elder sister Alice and her husband Chris Normal Actually. Chris and Alice think Giles and Emily are bloody soft, frankly, but more of that later.

Giles works in finance, but to be honest, things have been lean in the past couple of years. Giles still works hard, but is increasingly stressed, and there are far less perks than there used to be, so the enjoyment isn't there. Luckily they had put aside some money in the good times, but, well, put it this way, given the rises in school fees, if someone made them a decent offer for the second home in Southwold right now, they would snap their hand off. Thank God for M&S Wise Buys and the Boden catalogue, as Emily says to her close friends!

Emily is still really busy with the kids (James, 12, Madeleine, eight, and Ifor, four), although

Giles first met Emily at a corporate do

now they're a bit older they do more on their own; nowadays she just seems to be always taking them to places or picking them up from clubs/lessons/friends' houses. The kids have a busier social life than she does! She had to pack in the teaching assistant work, but she is heavily involved with the school PTA now; a couple of years ago she and a group of younger mums staged a little coup, basically, and have now completely revamped it. She knows damn well other mothers say they're cliquey, but the fact is no one else wants to do the hard work.

Emily and Giles's tastes are, for the most part, thoroughly contemporary. They swapped the Audi Allroad for a new Freelander, and just had to get a second car for Emily what with all the taxi-ing – she has a nice little A-Class now and it does her very

WHERE TO SPOT THE LIBERAL ACTUALLYS IN 2010

- On PTA of your child's school
- At Elton John concert, crying to *Candle in the Wind* if tipsy
- Corporate hospitality tent at Wimbledon
- Peter Jones bedding department
- Farmers' markets
- Cornwall (weekends & summer only)

Oh look, lemon curd!

THINGS YOU MIGHT EXPERIENCE AT GILES AND EMILY'S

- Extra-large wine glasses
- Entire wall devoted to holiday pictures
- Smell of damp country clothes drying
- Sound of Chris's laugh although he is 30 metres away at bottom of garden
- Corduroy
- Nuzzling from over-attentive Labrador

She loves visitors

SARACENS

Football's fun but they still love rugger

nicely! Giles remains a gadget nut, and gets very pleased when he manages to download snidey apps on to his iPhone (he's thinking about going back to Blackberry though – they seem more grown up). They had to buy some new computers for the kids' homework, and what with those and the Wii, Sky+ HD, and second espresso maker – the house is like a branch of bloody Dixons sometimes. As Chris says (gadgets are a major topic of conversation between he and his brother-in-law), it's all very well Giles getting disillusioned and talking about running a cheese business in bloody Pembrokeshire but the first time he loses the signal for the Ashes he'll have a fit.

Emily herself departs from her own elder peers' behaviour chiefly in respect of fashion; Emily likes to talk of herself as a bit of a fashionista, and loves to say

HOW THE LIBERAL ACTUALLYS AVOID ROWS WITH FRIENDS AT DINNER PARTIES

To stop their more youthful and democratic view of the world leading to rows with older relatives and friends, Emily and Giles devised a sign language to avoid awkward subjects.

Don't discuss banks; Chris was at school with chap from Goldman Sachs

May be OK to admit James is vegetarian – have just seen Riverford Organic box in kitchen

Watch it – he's nearly drunk that bottle of wine and it interferes with his knee-injury medication

Avoid immigration – he grew up in South Africa and thinks Mandela shouldn't have been freed

Don't compliment the crockery, it was his mother's and she hates it

If he talks about the biscuit game over pudding again, ignore him and hope she does same

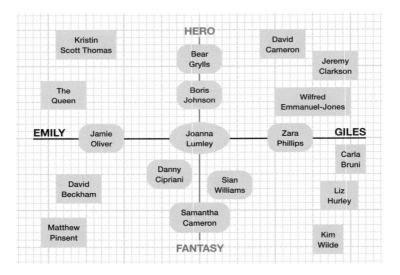

she is going to do *some serious shopping* at Westfield. She discovered *Sex in the City* quite late on, but made up for lost time by maxing out her Amex on Jimmy Choos and Manolos; she began buying *Vogue* again, which she had last done when at school in the 1980s, when they read it mainly to look for friends of friends in the party section at the back. Many of her friends have gone the same way, and they love to have a laugh about some of their old chums who still stick with the old Sloaney look. Mind you, they think some of the younger girls take it too far, and look trashy; not combing your bloody hair isn't a fashion statement, is it? Emily is perplexed to note that some of the younger set seem to be reverting; Kate Middleton looks such a bloody Sloane it's untrue, but then again she's an odd one – it's that mother.

WHEN TO MAKE A DECISION

Giles and Emily have suffered a sense of
dislocation and disillusion during the recession,
and realised that what they previously
considered very solid is actually quite fragile.
Their feelings about the future and ideas about
what else they could do often depend on how
bleak they are feeling.

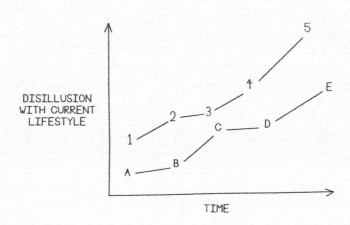

Giles
1 Start own investment business on radical
 new business model
2 Move to countryside an hour outside city
 and set up own wine merchant business
3 Set up cheese business in Pembrokeshire
4 Become organic farmer in Outer Hebrides
5 Live in Canadian woods and earn living from
 forestry and survival skills

Emily
A Take part-time job
B Open radical new child-centred nursery with
 Enid Blyton theme
C Move to countryside an hour outside city
D Downsize and do charity work
E Move back to countryside where she grew
 up and work in shop

HOW TO SPOT MR LIBERAL ACTUALLY

1. Navy crew-neck sweater
2. Pale blue cotton shirt
3. Faded blue polo shirt
4. Pale chinos (Gap)
5. Signet ring that looks too small for his doughty fingers
6. Tie conspicuous by its absence these days
7. Tweed shooting jacket
8. Short hair, appears to never grow
9. Black Converse All Star trainers in wardrobe, worn once
10. Scott hybrid bike

HOW TO SPOT MRS LIBERAL ACTUALLY

1. Wrap dresses in big bold prints
2. Brora cashmere jumper (M&S if feeling poorgeois)
3. LK Bennett shoes (Dune ditto)
4. Links' Sweetie bracelet
5. Ralph Lauren jeans (mud from dog walking around ankles)
6. Glossy shoulder-length hair
7. Knee-high boots
8. Coat from Boden
9. Ballet pumps
10. Sunny smile

Antique

Retro

In other words, although Giles and Emily's tastes are heartily British – they feel at home in places like the Home Counties and heart of England, they holiday in Celtic coastal places such Western Scotland, Cornwall and Wales – they are aware of a vague generation gap between themselves and some of their older relatives and friends, who they will often refer to as "old Sloanes". Nowadays, the Liberal Actuallys will do things that 20 years ago their families considered utterly feckless; to Chris and Alice's utter horror, they even went on an anti-war

HOW TO BE POORGEOIS

Dom P '68

M&S £7.99

Box at Chelsea

Sky+ box

South of France

Southwold

First class without thinking

EasyJet without blinking

Bottega Veneta

Boden

demo a few years ago ("Don't you know there's a rugby match on?" barked Alice down the phone, with no trace of irony).

They also do pop music. Chris still thinks a gig is something that horses pull, but Giles and Emily take a picnic to two or three heritage gigs every summer (they saw Bryan Ferry in concert in a forest last year – the man was superb). And they like football (which Chris considers somehow less authentic than rugger). They're season ticket holders at Arsenal (though to be honest they are not keen on matches against clubs sitting below halfway in the Premiership) and now that their local club has been promoted to the Premiership, they go to watch them, too. James has eight shirts in all, including home and away for Arsenal – sometimes he wears them all on matchdays, which makes Giles and Emily chuckle. What they really love at the Emirates is bumping into friends on the way, or at half time. It feels like being part of something magical.

All this means that the Liberal Actuallys now spend far more time in the presence of people who are less wealthy than themselves, and partly as a result they now have more of a social conscience than Chris and Alice. This can lead to arguments, such as the one about David Cameron and "the gays" (to be fair, Chris shouldn't have been drinking on top of the painkillers). They now try to avoid certain topics, concentrating instead on the kids (though not schools!) and dogs.

What of the future for the Liberal Actuallys? Giles talks now and again about just packing it all in and setting up that cheese business in Wales. So what if they had to send the kids to state school? Emily

SOCIAL NETWORKING WITH GILES AND EMILY

Emily Liberal–Actually 12 week old chocolate lab!

Favourite Dogs

 Sun at 14:54 · Comment · Like · Share

 Catherine Esher Looks just like Cadbury. We miss him.
Yesterday at 19:39

Justin Fleet Did I see you in the paddock with Merlin today? Sorry couldn't stop!
5 hours ago

Emily enjoys Facebook because it allows her to share all her pictures of the dogs. When she goes riding she sometimes adds pictures of the horses, too. She adds lots of pictures of the kids, but it is a close-run thing as to whether she adds more of them or of the two chocolate labs (Merlin and Dumbledore) and the Jack Russell (Lucy). She will also post pictures of friends' dogs and parents' dogs when she goes to visit. Emily is quite likely to get involved in Facebook chat, too.

Giles would not go near Facebook, as he is protective of his privacy and thinks he will have his details stolen. He does, however, know about Twitter, and has used it as part of a work initiative – he has no sense of it being fashionable or trendy, and thinks of it as something to be used by businesses rather than individuals. He is, of course, on LinkedIn. They both use Skype (with streaming video webcam) so their parents can see the grandchildren more often.

thinks he is going too far (but only tells her mother, who agrees).

Still, they could become more flexible because they've become used to having less money. They are pretty upfront about being poorer. For a while they tried to carry on as normal, but now they tend to opt for obvious denial, rather than trying to do the same things but cheaper. One of their mates whose in the same boat says they are all "poorgeois" or "poshtere" now, i.e almost proud of how austere they

THE LIBERAL ACTUALLY SUB-TRIBES

THE NORMAL ACTUALLYS

Chris and Alice. Live in similar capacious semi-detached house on outskirts of major conurbation, would like to move further out. Chris works in finance, Alice looks after children. Both traditionally minded and conservative with small and large Cs, and cannot abide political correctness or wetness. Think "it's about time somebody sorted this bloody country out".
Role models: Duke of Edinburgh & Camilla Parker Bowles

HI! GUYS

Ian and Helen. Live in detached house on edge of commuter town. Work in marketing and HR respectively. Watchword is "positive". "Working hard and playing harder" they project immense, American confidence and joy in living. Can appear to be almost constantly smiling and vigorously shaking hands.
Role models: Tom Ford & Meryl Streep

CONVERSATIVES

Xav and Jess. Live in flat in prosperous suburb, work in media. Progressive, fashion-conscious couple who combine considerable wealth with interests once associated with the liberal left, particularly green issues. Recently took year out to do voluntary work in Africa. Regarded with mutual suspicion by the Normal Actuallys.
Role models: Zac Goldsmith & Samantha Cameron

THE AUSSAUKUSA

Robin and Gila. Live in large flat in affluent urban area with much period architecture. Work for banks, married with two small children. Robin's Aussie, Gila South African, both Anglophiles, convinced that Great Britain is more civilised and cultured than home. Have many friends from old colonial countries, i.e Australia, South Africa, UK, USA, hence the name of their group.
Role models: Andrew Strauss & Cath Kidston

can be. The trick is to show how economical you can be while still maintaining good taste. "A bottle of M&S Cava when you have guests for dinner is fine," says Giles, "whereas a Tesco own-brand Champagne wouldn't be the same at all."

THE CHAVEAU RICHES

Scott and Tash grew up on the London-Kent borders. Scott's dad worked selling insurance until the late 1980s, when he spotted a gap in the market for a new product, and made his family very rich. Tash's mum and dad have split up, but her dad has a building firm and her mum runs a small chain of beauty/tanning salons. Scott went to a comprehensive, Tash's mum scraped enough together to send her to a small private school – neither was a conspicuous academic success, but they were far from being bad kids; just middling, as they say. The fact that none of the teachers at their school predicted they would do so well for themselves makes them quite proud, in a way.

Scott started off as a dj, then set up a dj agency and now has his fingers in all sorts of pies; he has a dance show touring theatres all over the South East, has gone into partnership with a property dealer, and has this new scheme he ain't telling anyone about except to say he's down to the last selection round on *Dragons' Den*. Tash tried a bit of modelling but then buckled down and helped her mum with the

They had it specially made

salons, and began looking into surgery, dentistry, stuff like that. They have. Made. A. Bomb. Her and her mum row and fall out, but they keep it together and now own 12 salons, and employ 40 girls. Some of them can be right lazy little so-and-sos though, only wanting to talk about where they're going this Friday. You have to watch them like a hawk.

They first met when someone Scott worked with got in touch to ask if they could do make-up for the dancers at one of his gigs. It went from there, basically. They are not married – ain't got time, mate, too much to do! – but when they do, it will cost a vast amount of money and have a fairy-tale theme. Weddings are very, very important for the Chaveau Riches, because they are a reason to create a material fantasy world, and Scott and Tash adore

HOW BIG IS YOUR SOFA?

Scott and Tash really like big things, especially if the things are connected with leisure, pleasure or entertainment. If it's a real feature piece, they'll look into getting it custom-made – you'll never regret something like that because it's unique to you. Beds, sofas, lawns, cushions, TV, speakers, barbecue, cars – all of it needs to be as large as possible. They intend to own a Hummer one day, and are intrigued by Sharp's new 70" TV.

Scott has meaningful tattoos

fantasy, although they don't necessarily talk about it as such (to be honest, Scott and Tash tend to think of "fantasy" as a sexual term if anything, sex also being very important).

They aim to have a baby soon, so they have been planning a fabulous nursery with the aid of an architect. There is plenty of room – they live together in a new five-bedroom house which is furnished in a sort of British version of the Los Angeles style commonly seen on *Cribs* (they love *Cribs*). This is a blend, rarely seen in mainstream furnishing magazines, of modern minimalist mixed with extravagant opulence; anything soft or to do with entertainment is massive – beds, sofas, lawns, cushions, TV, speakers, barbecue – while everything with a function (which automatically makes it feel a

THE CHAVEAU RICHES' HEROES AND VILLAINS

OMG?

WTF?

EWW

Katie Price
Mariah Carey
Elton John
Snoop Dogg
Abbey Clancy
Dannii Minogue
Alex Meraz
Angelina Jolie
Peter Andre
Amy Winehouse
The Cruises
Kerry Katona
Robbie Williams
Kanye West
Victoria Beckham
George Monbiot
Johnny Vegas
Harriet Harman

**THINGS SCOTT
& TASH SAY**

That's major

Loves it!

Whatevs

Perf

Gorge

OMG

bit boring and irksome, because you have less control over where you can put it) is sleek and minimal. There are lots of gadgets – Scott loves them – and a room done out in a pink, girly style with chiffon clouds attached to ceiling. They used to live half their lives in nightclubs, but nowadays they don't get out all that much apart from to work-related functions; instead they have friends round all the time, and are generous in the extreme. Social creatures at heart, the Chaveaus have a strong urge to share the benefits of their money. "Money is only a means to an end, you have to keep hold of that," as they told the reporter from the local glossy homes-and-lifestyle magazine.

Essentially their style is that of the contemporary High Celebrity age, but it is not so much that they take their cues from *OK*, *Cribs* and Jordan – it is more

HOW THE CHAVEAU RICHES GET MARRIED PT1

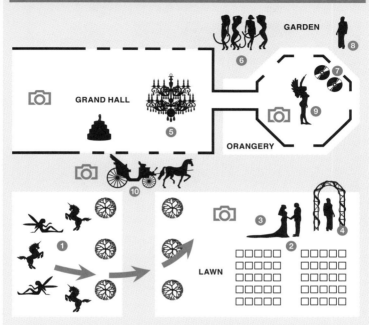

1   Unicorns (Shetland ponies with horns attached) and wood sprites (child actors)

2   Happy couple during ceremony

3   Presiding official

4   Opera singer hired to do *Pie Jesu* when happy couple exchange the rings

5   Construction featuring flowers and fairylights around and over head table, inspired by the bandstand at end of *Twilight*

6   Four podiums with fantasy dancers, outfits based on the *Avatar* movie

7   Big-name professional dj booth

8   Opera singer singing again at 11pm

9   Semi-erotic ice sculpture; Tash's outrageous friend Suki will cause outrage and appal Scott's mother at 11.30pm by pretending to rub the nipple on it

10 Carriage drawn by unicorns (large horses this time, the pièce de résistance) to carry away happy couple, after mild panic when Scott cannot be found because he is trying to defuse row between best man and best man's wife

HOW THE CHAVEAU RICHES GET MARRIED PT2

Water features made the venue seem like fairyland

The page boys' cupid outfits were awesome

The maypole took it to the next level

that they share the same values. At the heart of these values is a fantasy version of what old Hollywood glamour would have been like, which is where the fantasy comes in. Their devotion to fantasy tells you something important about them. They grew up in the long boom when there seemed so much of everything and yet all the money still left you stuck in the Home Counties with their rain and traffic jams and ugly miserable-looking people.

Even all the individual success couldn't transform the entire world – and so they began transforming their own little bit of it. Sometimes it is as if the actual world can't give either of them the excitement they feel it should; they would, ideally, like to feel as if they were living in a film, and to get closer to that they have some crazy ideas about what they would

WHAT TASH TALKS ABOUT AT WORK

SCAMS INVOLVING BOGUS EAST EUROPEAN COSMETIC SURGERY PROCEDURES

HOLIDAYS SHE AND MEMBERS OF STAFF ARE PLANNING

INTERESTING BOOKS SHE IS READING ABOUT SPIRITUALITY

KATIE PRICE

HOW ANNOYING NEGATIVE PEOPLE ARE

HOW ANNOYING HER MOTHER CAN BE

WAYS OF EXPANDING BUSINESS

MEMBERS OF STAFF'S NEW HAIR AND MAKE-UP IDEAS

like to do with the house – creating fairy wonderlands and caves and all sorts. As yet they just have Tash's girly room – but wait until you see those amazing plans for the nursery!

When Scott and Tash get fed up, they sometimes think about moving to Jersey where Scott's uncle lives – life is pretty good there, you have to say.

They get sick of all the moaners and the bullshit in England; too many dolescum scrounging, too much negativity, too many people everywhere creaming off money without producing anything of any value, and too much looking backwards. Because they are just about still in touch with their families' working-class origins – something they are prone to exaggerate – they think of themselves as entirely self-made people who have struggled really

CUSTOM PLATES

Tash and Scott bought each other their private plates not long after they had moved in together. They both love them – the plates are a laugh, of course, but in a way they are also about tightening the bond between themselves and their cars. Tash and Scott love their cars (sporty for him, roomy 4x4 for her), and in some ways feel most at ease when driving – hence, in part, wanting to stamp the car with their own identity.

hard and worked for every penny; like TV talent show contestants, they incorporate into their own stories an element of the rags-to-riches hero from Hollywood musicals.

The recession has been kind to them – their businesses thrive regardless – and so Scott and Tash go on consuming and imagining. In many ways, Scott and Tash are the embodiment of the great consumerist, individualist energy that was set loose in the 1980s. Back then, some commentators thought the energy would transform the whole country; it didn't, but it meant that some enormous gardens would look like Narnia for millionaires.

As Scott and Tash demonstrate, this energy could also be more fair and generous than it is sometimes given credit for. The Chaveau Riches are more open-minded than many of the tribes who make a show of their liberal credentials: their friends are more varied than The Hornby Set (Page 25); they are more fiercely protective of their families than Jamie Oliver's Army (Page 15) and they are less uptight than White Vain Man (Page 72). They work

THE CHAVEAU RICHES SUB-TRIBES

SUBURBERRYS

Steve and Mandi. Live in detached house in commuter belt of large city. Steve owns a building company, Mandi does books. Strong family bonds, though children in teens/early 20s can be wayward. Love holidays (including the airport) and the garden, and have recently got really into their wine. Deeply annoyed by Gordon Brown, glad he's gone.
Role models: Pam & Mick Shipman

TOYTOWN TYCOONS

Al & Kelli. Live in large detached house with large garden on affluent city-edges. Al senior partner in golf-course chain. Kelli has own fledgling yoga-wear line. Very wealthy, but aside from large house and luxury cars, spend on "fun" rather than to project "classiness". Garden has permanent bouncy castle; home has pamper-room and signed Beatles artefacts on display.
Role models: Chris Evans & Natasha Shishmanian

QATAR PLAYERS

David and Claire. Live in detached company property in prosperous town in green belt. Live in fear of being relocated to Aberdeen or similar. David works for American multinat involved in primary industries, spends much time in the Middle East. Claire corporate wife. Own large expensive items in which they seem to have little interest. David happily rootless. Claire ambivalent.
Role models: Mark Thatcher & Sarah Russell

FOXTONS FORCE FIVE

Jay & Preena. Live in one-bedroom flat in new housing development in outer suburb. Work for estate agents, but despite junior status manage to stretch income and credit so that their possessions, leisure interests suggest considerable and impressive wealth. New haircut every week, pointy shoes, will own Porsche by 2020.
Role models: Any winner from The Apprentice, Raef Bjayou & Michelle Dewberry

very, very hard and they believe in giving everyone – *everyone* – a fair chance. And in many ways, they are more open-minded and egalitarian than any other tribe in this book.

THE ALT.MIDDLES

Finally we come to an unusual and rather lost middle-class tribe, which happens to be the one with the most diverse members.

The alt.middles are a friendly but confused bunch of people. Outwardly, they may well belong to one of the groups we've described in the earlier chapters, but inside they find it impossible to buy into things with the same enthusiasm as their friends. On hen-weekends, the alt.middle woman is the one suffering visible embarrassment at the idea of being "pampered". At the football, alt.middle man is more depressed by the sight of wine being sold in the refreshments bar than by his club losing. At corporate away days, or during PowerPoint presentations in the office, they may have to leave the room to sob helplessly. People say: "Cheer up, alt.middle – it might never happen!" To which the alt.middle replies, "But it *is* happening! Now! All around us! And people saying, 'cheer up it might never happen' are part of 'it' 'happening'!"

Alt.middles can be any age, and might do any job, although they are unlikely to crop up in positions for

A special kind of misery

which unqualified enthusiasm is needed. Politically, they are inclined to be liberal and open-minded about race, class and gender, but they have a sceptical view of politicians that makes them open to conspiracy theories. They find it far easier, for example, to believe in rumours about the 9/11 attacks or Diana's death than in a politician or CEO's claim to care about people's welfare.

They don't feel a terribly strong affiliation to any sort of group or organisation, and many share Groucho Marx's sentiments – the only groups they even begin to admire are made up of people who they assume would dislike them. They do have, luckily for them, a great ability to seek each other out as if by radar. At weddings, the alt.middles of all ages tend to gather in one or two groups, gradually gaining the wine-enhanced confidence to ask each other if they didn't think the décor a bit overdone and choice of first song cringey? It is in these rare moments of bonhomie with strangers and pals that alt.middles feel all is not yet lost for the world, and think that actually, they are not in such a minority as

131

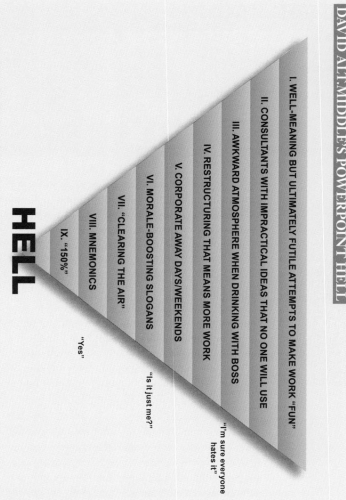

DAVID ALT.MIDDLE'S POWERPOINT HELL

I. WELL-MEANING BUT ULTIMATELY FUTILE ATTEMPTS TO MAKE WORK "FUN"

II. CONSULTANTS WITH IMPRACTICAL IDEAS THAT NO ONE WILL USE

III. AWKWARD ATMOSPHERE WHEN DRINKING WITH BOSS

IV. RESTRUCTURING THAT MEANS MORE WORK

V. CORPORATE AWAY DAYS/WEEKENDS

VI. MORALE-BOOSTING SLOGANS

VII. "CLEARING THE AIR"

VIII. MNEMONICS

IX. "150%"

HELL

"Yes"

"Is it just me?"

"I'm sure everyone hates it"

THE ALT.MIDDLE GAZE

An easy way to spot an alt.middle is to look for the alt.middle gaze. This is a look of blank horror adopted when confronting middle-class absurdities that ought to be seen as evidence of insanity, but which are accepted by those around them. It involves freezing your face in the closest you can get to a smile, and looking fixedly into the middle-distance. "Am I the only one who finds this situation ridiculous?" it says. "Oh God – yes I am." Alt.middle exponents include Charlie Brown, Tim and Dawn in *The Office*, and Sue and Pete in *Outnumbered*.

A leading exponent of the gaze

Of course it's the original

they think (they wonder a lot about whether they are in a minority or not; sometimes they secretly think they have something wrong with them). Sadly, these experiences always end the same way; they fall asleep feeling happy, and then they wake up to find Katy Perry is number one again, the TV ads targeted at women seem to have got worse, and so their despair springs afresh.

As these attitudes cross groups and ages it is in some ways pointless to outline a typical couple, but a representative one is David and Kate, in their mid-thirties, living in a 1930s semi-detached suburban house which they have decorated roughly in keeping with the period (rough historical integrity is a middle way through "contemporary" naffness and the showiness of classic or modern antique styling). The

OMG WTF?!?!

Online, alt.middles cringe at acronyms such as lol and rofl, and rarely if ever use emoticons – probably because such devices suggest simple, direct thoughts, and the alt.middle tends to feel ambivalent about most things. Useful acronyms for David and Kate would be:

AITOOWFTSR?
Am I the only one who finds this situation ridiculous?

ITWLHCT?
Is this what life has come to?

IIWMDIWKY
If I was more decisive, I would kill you

Alt.middles never use an emoticon, but if they did it would look like this:

house is in the mid-suburbs, not particularly close to town, and near a decent-sized park. They live as a couple but are unmarried, and are going to start a family in the next year or so. David is the deputy head of English in a good comprehensive, Kate is a barrister for a firm specialising in employment law – her work requires her to be very tough and resolute, but she doesn't often talk about it. They are interested in a wide variety of subjects, though he thinks some of her telly just too girly. He watches reality shows claiming that she makes him, but actually places bets on contestants because he thinks he can analyse the public's tastes semi-scientifically. She finds some of the stuff he records from BBC Four dull beyond belief. ("Yes, it *is* interesting that the Moog led to so much interesting music. But a whole hour on how it was invented, Dave?")

When it comes to shopping and lifestyle tastes, David and Kate's desire to distance themselves from the mainstream leads to a fondness for obscure, nostalgic and vintage things. Their ideal car, if they have kids, is an old Volvo 245DL estate. Sadly, for

DAVID & KATE DEEPLY APPRECIATE

Michelle Obama: attracts rare feelings of unqualified love and admiration

Dizzee Rascal: though they fear their embrace might ultimately destroy him

Ruth Jones

Arcade Fire

Bill Murrray

Richard Dawkins

Alan Johnson

Florence Welch

Rio Ferdinand

ANTI-SOCIAL NETWORKING WITH THE ALT.MIDDLES

 Likes the idea but can't think of anything good to say

 Enjoys long discussions of trivial items; bewildered by popularity of the games

 LinkedIn makes them wish they were unemployed

 Perversely enjoyed it going wrong when a media mogul bought it

 Cheered by old schoolfriends who remind him/her of innocent days before the hell of modern adulthood

 Chatroulette? You must be joking.

them, the High Street has caught up with their period-style-decorated home in recent years, and almost everything the alt.middles have used to personalise their homes in the past 40 years is now on sale at a chain store, from 1930s Coca-Cola signs, to hand-stitched wall hangings made from scraps of saris, to prints of Edvard Munch's *The Scream* to *Keep Calm and Carry On* signs.

They hate this, and increasingly find themselves choosing or liking things or people purely on the grounds that they have not been co-opted by a big brand yet. They often quite like things simply because they're non-mainstream; when David said he wasn't keen on Florence Welch, Kate pointed out that "at least she's not Katy f***ing Perry", which was enough to persuade him.

It has to be said, though, that despite their long-standing objections to the bland corporate mainstream, David and Kate, like all alt.middles, are becoming a little more tolerant of the sort of Americanised, smiley-happy service culture they find in places like, say, Pret A Manger or boutique

COULD YOU BE AN ALT.MIDDLE?

Many people in other middle-class groups eventually turn into alt.middles, and others spend years combining the qualities of both alt.middle-ism and their original tribe. Could you be a prospective convert? Likely candidates include:

THE LOFT WINGERS who find they're beginning to dislike their friends

THE DAMN-WRIGHTS who have lost the will to fight back

THE LIBERAL ACTUALLYS who drift off during meetings

THE CHAVEAU RICHES who wonder why their parents seemed happier than them

THE FAIR TO MIDDLINGS who feel an increasingly strong yet vague sense of guilt

JAMIE OLIVER'S ARMY members who feel disenchanted with their employer

THE JACK PACK who are finding it hard to maintain their sense of humour

THE CAN-DO!S on anti-depressants

THE HORNBY SETS disillusioned with politics

WHITE VAIN MEN & NO SUGAR BABES who don't enjoy shopping like they used to

hotels. After all, it is better than the rage and violence lurking beneath the surface of much of the British retail experience; surely it is preferable to be told to have a nice day by someone who doesn't mean it than to be aggressively ignored then patronised by someone who does?

Alt.middles would love to have answers to all this, but knowing they don't have them, and feeling the country to be bereft of ideas and leaders, they lapse into consoling nostalgia and emigration fantasies, devouring books by David Kynaston and David Peace, and enrolling the kids in Mandarin classes. Sometimes it's hard to know whether they are hopeless idealists, or just plain grumpy, but on the whole it's safe to say they believe in a better world. They're just not sure where it is.

WHICH TRIBE ARE YOU?

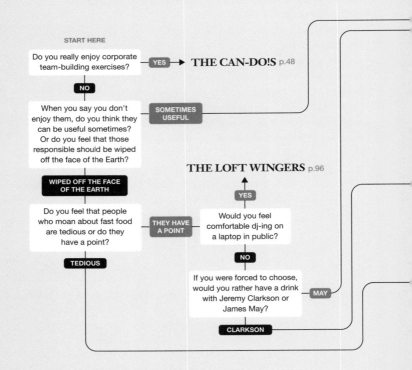

START HERE

Do you really enjoy corporate team-building exercises? → **YES** → **THE CAN-DO!S** p.48

NO

When you say you don't enjoy them, do you think they can be useful sometimes? Or do you feel that those responsible should be wiped off the face of the Earth? → **SOMETIMES USEFUL**

WIPED OFF THE FACE OF THE EARTH

THE LOFT WINGERS p.96

Do you feel that people who moan about fast food are tedious or do they have a point? → **THEY HAVE A POINT** → Would you feel comfortable dj-ing on a laptop in public? → **YES**

NO

TEDIOUS

If you were forced to choose, would you rather have a drink with Jeremy Clarkson or James May? → **MAY**

CLARKSON

A table showing the relationships between the tribes described in this book and more than 50 others can be found at www.middleclasshandbook.co.uk

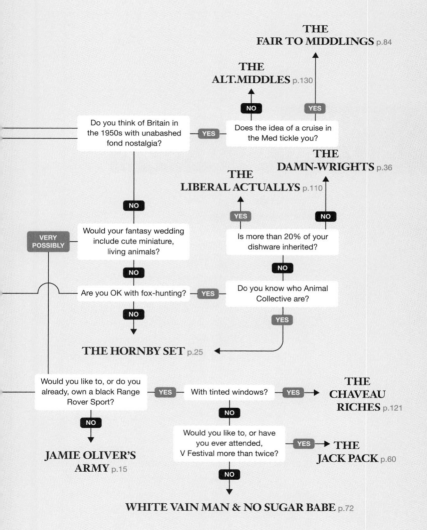

THE
FAIR TO MIDDLINGS p.84

THE
ALT.MIDDLES p.130

Do you think of Britain in the 1950s with unabashed fond nostalgia? — YES → Does the idea of a cruise in the Med tickle you?

NO

YES

THE
DAMN-WRIGHTS p.36

THE
LIBERAL ACTUALLYS p.110

YES

NO

Would your fantasy wedding include cute miniature, living animals?

VERY POSSIBLY

Is more than 20% of your dishware inherited?

NO

NO

Are you OK with fox-hunting? — YES → Do you know who Animal Collective are?

NO

YES

THE HORNBY SET p.25

Would you like to, or do you already, own a black Range Rover Sport? — YES → With tinted windows? — YES → THE CHAVEAU RICHES p.121

NO

NO

Would you like to, or have you ever attended, V Festival more than twice? — YES → THE JACK PACK p.60

JAMIE OLIVER'S ARMY p.15

NO

WHITE VAIN MAN & NO SUGAR BABE p.72

ABOUT
NOT ACTUAL SIZE

Not Actual Size is a London-based group of people that explores the big meanings of small things, both in its own creative projects and work for clients, who currently include Nike, Ray-Ban and the V&A.

Our own projects, like *The Middle Class Handbook*, seek to consider aspects of modern life in Britain with intelligence and humour, teasing out the wider significance in the minutiae of the mundane. Our commercial work entails creating content for brands that will entertain people, and allows them to see their own lives reflected in the brand's media. The content can be used directly by brands, or their PR or advertising agencies, or sold into the media by Not Actual Size itself. Much of our recent work has been online, but we also produce books and films, and stage events.

As a company, Not Actual Size believes that if companies want people to develop a relationship with them, they need content that can start and sustain conversations about subjects knitted into people's lives. Obviously that content must be related to the brand, but it works best when it has integrity

CLASS OF 2004/05

The first book

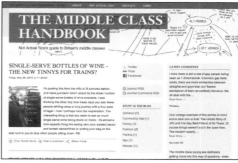

www.middleclasshandbook.co.uk

and desirability in its own right. We feel the best way to achieve that is simply to work with creative people who have experience of creating successful, attractive, compelling content that works in its own right – which is why we employ respected creatives from journalism, television, the arts and academia to produce unique content.

The Not Actual Size approach involves two steps. Firstly using researchers, who combine academic methodologies with a populist sensibility, and secondly turning this raw material into entertainment that both demonstrates brand values and gets people interested. Our specialism is talking to people about the wonder of everyday experiences. We have, for example, produced award-winning work based on such commonplace activities as using mobile phones, eating fast food, and commuting by car. These subjects are not glamorous – not usually, anyway – but people have strong feelings and ideas about them, and they enjoy sharing those feelings and ideas with each other.

The vital point is that the conduit between the

The Secret Life of Cars for BMW   *How to be Abducted by Aliens* for Grolsch

small things and the big meaning is PEOPLE. It is people alone who can transform the mundane into the momentous and, as *The Middle Class Handbook* tries to show, that is surely something we are all trying to do, in our own way.

CREDITS & ACKNOWLEDGEMENTS

Devised & Directed by Not Actual Size

Edited by Stephen Armstrong and Richard Benson
for Not Actual Size

Designed by Fibre

Thanks to

Stephen Armstrong, Joy Asibey, Dean Barrett, Guy Benson,
Pauline Benson, Alex Bilmes, Sam Blunden, Kevin Braddock,
Matt Brooke, Frances Brown, Christina Bunce, Donna Clarke,
Gareth Coombs, Hector Coombs, Laura Craik, Stephen Cross,
Karen Dacre, John Edmondson, Dave Dyett, Patrick Fry,
Preena Gadher, Katy Glen, Henrietta Cripps, Anna Guyer,
Mark Harrison, Kenneth Hill, Amy Hitchenor, Will Hogan,
Dan Holliday, Rachel Holmes, Anwen Hooson, Kyle Huggall,
Lucy Hyslop, Jennifer Kabat, Rob Lands, Wrisley Magargal,
Jessica Mayne, Simon Mills, Sean Moore, Ken Morrison,
Jon Myers, Ben Newman, Ben Pollard, Mark Poppenborg,
David Rainbird, Sarah Raphael, Mark Ratcliff, Barney Ronay,
Julian Rudd, Miranda Sawyer, Sheila Speed, Spellman,
Adam Thomas, Gill Thornton, Emma Thornton, Vanda Varga,
Issy Wells, Justine Wells, Theresa Wells, Kevin Welsh,
Nicola Welsh, Nina Whitby, Geoff Widdop and Billy Woods.

p54 rain dance by craig Cloutier, Flickr CC BY-SA
p58 *Modbury Bags* by Sally Parkinson
     Synch festival official products, Sampler bag, designed by Serena
     Galdo, www.synch.gr
p59 *Turtle string bags* by Heatheronhertravels.com, Flickr
     I'm NOT a Smug Twat Bag by marissa v, Flickr
     M&S bag: *passion for tote bags* by kaylovesvintage, Flickr
p60 *Vision* by Adrian Boliston, Flickr CC BY
p61 *13/365: 1/13/09 - Credit Crunch* by KristyR929, Flickr
p62 *Three Stripes* by Kick Photo, Flickr CC BY-ND
p63 *Brooklyn Bridge, NYC* by Francisco Diez, Flickr CC BY
p65 *Cancun Beach 3* by Abir Anwar, Flickr CC BY
     Kombo Beach Hotel by Victoria Reay, Flickr CC BY
     Stray Dog on the beach by Henning Leweke, Flickr CC BY-SA
     The Beach by Keith Parker, Flickr CC BY-SA
     Egypt 2008 by Shamil Khakirov, Flickr CC BY-SA
     Sarimsakli parasols by Filip Maljković, Flickr CC BY-SA
p68 *Gordon Ramsey* by mindspiker, Flickr CC BY-ND
p72 *2005 July Barn & rose blossom* by Vicki Clemerson, Flickr
p73 *It Just Works* by Gareth Simpson, Flickr CC BY
p74 Megan Fox by pinguino k, Flickr CC BY
     Angelina Jolie by Stefan Servos, Wikimedia Commons CC BY-SA
     Beyoncé Knowles by Chrisa Hickey, Wikimedia Commons CC BY
     Rihanna by AnnaPitton, Flickr CC BY-SA
     José Mourinho by Steindy, Wikimedia Commons CC BY-SA
     Lewis Hamilton by AngMoKio, Wikimedia Commons CC BY-SA
     Hugh Jackman by Grant Brummett, Wikimedia Commons CC BY-SA
p76 *Basset Hound* by Lilly M, Wikimedia Commons CC BY-SA
     Mojito by Jean-Philippe Rebuffet, Flickr
p77 *Shoes: hard work* by Valentina, Flickr CC BY
p79 *Breitling Navitimer Wrist* by Craig Billingsley, Flickr
p85 Ferrero Rocher by *Zoha.N, Flickr CC BY
     Crystal and Chrysanthemums 1 by Suvodeb Banerjee, Flickr CC BY
     Bombay Sapphire by Jacob Munk-Stander, Flickr CC BY
     Swiss Army Knife by Dave Taylor, Flickr CC BY
p86 *Captain Jack Sparrow* by Michi1308, Flickr CC BY-SA
p87 Joanna Lumley by Liberal Democrats, Flickr CC BY-ND
     Lady GaGa by Danielåhskarlsson, Wikimedia Commons CC BY-SA
p89 Hollyhock: USDA-NRCS PLANTS Database / Britton, N.L., and
     A. Brown. 1913. *An illustrated flora of the northern United States,*
     Canada and the British Possessions. Vol. 2: 516.
     Chives: USDA-NRCS PLANTS Database / Britton, N.L., and A. Brown.
     1913. *An illustrated flora of the northern United States, Canada and*
     the British Possessions. Vol. 1: 497.
     Poppy: USDA-NRCS PLANTS Database / Britton, N.L., and A. Brown.
     1913. *An illustrated flora of the northern United States, Canada and*
     the British Possessions. Vol. 2: 137.
     Nasturtium: twistedNasturtiums by Jennifer Fleming
     Conifer: USDA-NRCS PLANTS Database / Britton, N.L., and A.
     Brown. 1913. *An illustrated flora of the northern United States,*

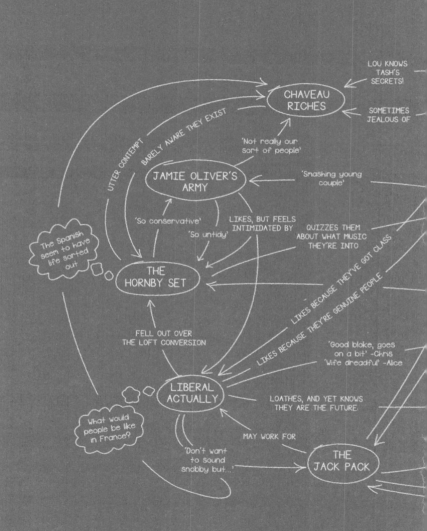